D0881905

"If the alarmingly challenged church in the Western world would imbibe the wisdom of this book, with its deeply biblical and engagingly practical articulation of the kingdom or reign of God, a renewed church could be birthed. This could well be Paul Stevens's most foundational and challenging book. It may well become a manifesto for a new Reformation."

—Charles Ringma
Regent College, emeritus

"This book is the result of a lifelong reflection and faithful journey to serve God 'full-time' in his kingdom. . . . Paul offers a kingdom perspective for the flourishing of the church, businesses, and Christian organizations. The church is the outcropping of the kingdom, business is a mission field, and the teachings of the Beatitudes are as relevant for the church as they are for business."

—Clive Lim
Regent College

"A kingdom view is essential for all Christians who strive to live faithfully in Christ. *The Kingdom of God in Working Clothes* gives a rich perspective of the scope of the reign of God and the place of the marketplace Christian within. It challenges us not only to live out kingdom values but to properly see the church missionally as a community of kingdom people. A must-read for all."

—Jean Lee
China Graduate School of Theology

"Paul is no doubt a pioneer in faith and work. This book has integrated the various dimensions of faith and work with the kingdom perspective, articulating the very presence of our King in the work, worker, and workplace. A must-read for everyone who wants to make sense of everyday work and how that may advance the kingdom."

—**Natalie Chan**
Bethel Bible Seminary

"The kingdom of God is the grand story from the beginning to the end. This book is leading us to reconnect our stories in the current marketplace to the grand story by integrating our faith and work. We, in all parts of the business and industries, realize that we have been already working in the kingdom, should be inspired to be working for the kingdom investment, and are supposed to be working as the embodied kingdom."

—**Andre Chen**
Global CEO, Denham Jeans

The Kingdom of God in Working Clothes

The Kingdom of God *in* Working Clothes

The Marketplace and the Reign of God

R. PAUL STEVENS

Foreword by Tom Nelson

CASCADE *Books* · Eugene, Oregon

THE KINGDOM OF GOD IN WORKING CLOTHES
The Marketplace and the Reign of God

Copyright © 2022 R. Paul Stevens. All rights reserved. Except for brief quotations in critical publications or reviews, no part of this book may be reproduced in any manner without prior written permission from the publisher. Write: Permissions, Wipf and Stock Publishers, 199 W. 8th Ave., Suite 3, Eugene, OR 97401.

Cascade Books
An Imprint of Wipf and Stock Publishers
199 W. 8th Ave., Suite 3
Eugene, OR 97401

www.wipfandstock.com

PAPERBACK ISBN: 978-1-6667-2515-5
HARDCOVER ISBN: 978-1-6667-2043-3
EBOOK ISBN: 978-1-6667-2044-0

Cataloguing-in-Publication data:

Names: Stevens, R. Paul, author.

Title: The kingdom of God in working clothes : the marketplace and the reign of God / R. Paul Stevens.

Description: Eugene, OR: Cascade Books, 2022 | Includes bibliographical references.

Identifiers: ISBN 978-1-6667-2515-5 (paperback) | ISBN 978-1-6667-2043-3 (hardcover) | ISBN 978-1-6667-2044-0 (ebook)

Subjects: LCSH: Laity. | Lay ministry. | Christian life.

Classification: BV4400 .S718 2022 (paperback) | BV4400 (ebook)

VERSION NUMBER 080222

All Scripture quotations, unless otherwise indicated, are taken from the Holy Bible, New International Version®, NIV®. Copyright ©2011 by Biblica, Inc.™ Used by permission of Zondervan. All rights reserved worldwide. www.zondervan.com. The "NIV" and "New International Version" are trademarks registered in the United States Patent and Trademark Office by Biblica, Inc.™

Contents

Foreword

by Tom Nelson

CONFESSION MAY BE GOOD for the soul, but it is hard for pastors. Several years into my pastoral ministry, I came to the painful conclusion that I was committing pastoral malpractice. Because of an impoverished theology and a resulting distorted pastoral vocational paradigm, I was spending the majority of my time equipping my congregation for the minority of their lives. Transparently, I was much more concerned how well I was doing on Sunday than how my parishioners were doing on Monday. Sadly, there was a large Sunday to Monday gap in my theological thinking and pastoral practice. Like many pastors, I had bought into an unbiblical dualism that elevated some work over other work. I had been looking through the murky lens of a sacred-secular dichotomy rather than a seamless kingdom vision. The negative consequences of my pastoral malpractice both in the spiritual formation of my congregation and its marketplace deployment for kingdom mission now make me shudder and cling to the mercy of God.

It has been astutely observed that the sacred secular dichotomy is one of the most pernicious and ubiquitous heresies of the church today. Paul Stevens not only shatters this false dichotomy, he also carves out an inviting path forward to a more integral, seamless, and God-honoring faith. Bringing together the strong theological themes of the kingdom, the priesthood of believers, and a robust vocational missiology, Paul Stevens persuasively strips away the painfully stubborn barnacles of an unbiblical dualism. Drawing from his deep reservoir of theological reflection and extensive life experience, he opens our eyes and hearts to see the good, true, and beautiful integral kingdom life available to us in every nook and cranny of life.

With a welcoming posture of humble confidence and hopeful realism, Paul Stevens paints a compelling picture of the already but not yet kingdom life in Christ available to us in our everyday Monday worlds. With skillful literary hands, he speaks with both a timely and timeless prophetic clarity. *"Kingdom work unifies everything we do in the home, marketplace, or educational institution into a sacrament, a means of bringing grace into the world and to people for the common good and that through down-to-earth work—the kingdom of God in working clothes"* (quoted in chapter 5).

Perhaps Paul Stevens's greatest contribution in narrowing the perilous Sunday to Monday gap may well be his persuasive apologetic for the primacy of the marketplace in the mission of God. The parallels between the first century and the twenty-first century are truly striking. The Pax Romana, however coercive, did make for a broader stability in the first-century world. Along with the Pax Romana was Rome's vast roadbuilding enterprise that made travel, communication, and commerce more dynamic and far-reaching. It was in this broader first-century milieu at the intersection of the marketplace where the gospel of the kingdom advanced in remarkable ways. Today in the twenty-first century with the Internet and the global economy, the world has never been more connected at the intersection of the marketplace. In my congregation it is more common for parishioners to interact in their workplace on Monday with a co-worker in India than it is for them to interact with someone who lives in the same city or a neighbor down the street. Yet in much of our mission thinking and strategy we are virtually ignoring the importance of equipping the scattered church for their global Monday marketplace worlds. *The Kingdom of God in Working Clothes* may just be the catalyst we so desperately need to move the twenty-first century apprentice of Jesus to be more on mission in the global marketplace.

The psalmist of old compares a wise life to a flourishing tree planted by streams of life-giving water that bears its fruit in its season. In this season of his life, it is more than evident that Paul Stevens is bearing much fruit that will remain for decades to come. Through his writings, Paul Stevens continues to be a tall tree of truth, grace, and wisdom on the Evangelical horizon. As a pastor who has had to come to grips with an impoverished theology and the resultant pastoral malpractice that accompanied my early years of church leadership, I only wish I could have read this fine book many years earlier.

This may well be Paul Stevens's finest work. Turning the pages I found myself echoing the words of the wine steward at a famous wedding in Cana long ago. *"But you have kept the good wine until now."* Don't rush through this book. Take your time and savor the fine wine of seasoned wisdom, the rich bouquet of theological reflection and tones of down-to-earthiness informing faithful kingdom living in the marketplace. No matter where you are in your spiritual journey, *The Kingdom of God In Working Clothes* will move you down the path of a more joyful, fulfilling, God-honoring integral life and mission in the world.

Introduction

AT THIRTY-EIGHT YEARS OF age I literally put on working clothes. I pulled on my jeans, bought industrial grade boots with metal toes, got a hard hat and a nail belt, and started to apprentice as a carpenter in a small home-building and renovation company in Vancouver. I had been building things since I was just old enough to hold a tool. I had built a boat each year of my teen years, not to mention furniture, but this was something else. I was clearly out of my depth. I had to pray a lot before making saw cuts on expensive California redwood lumber. I think I prayed more as a carpenter than I ever did as a pastor. I had been pastoring a wonderful church in Vancouver that hosted hundreds of students from the local university and lots of young working adults. It was a life dream to be there. But then over the period of a year God placed in my heart and that of my wife, Gail, another call—to work in the world. It was not a call "out of the blue."

Some of My Story as a Kingdom Person

I had become a follower of Jesus ten days before entering university. Immediately I felt that I wanted to serve God "full time." So I prepared myself for missionary service or pastoral work. Sadly there was no one in my life at the time to tell me I did not need to become a pastor in order to serve God "full time." Though I have no regrets from my life, and though I soon learned that there is no part-time option for followers of Jesus, I really had little experience of work in the world, what we are here calling the kingdom of God in working clothes. But it was not an easy transition on other fronts.

"You have left the ministry," my pastor friends taunted me. In contrast my wife and my parents were wonderfully supportive. The church I was serving did not fully understand my sense of calling even when, as a tentmaking pastor, I helped plant a crazy church among the many thousands of young adults that crowded into Vancouver in the summer of that year, sleeping mostly on the beaches. "You have left the ministry," friends joined the chant. But, I insisted, I am still ministering in the kingdom of God as well as the church. Eventually I bought into the business and became a carpenter and manager combo. I did this for several years, never expecting to write a book on the kingdom of God in working clothes.

The clothes of course change with the work done: sweatpants for the physical education teacher at the local high school, three-piece pinstripe suit for the downtown lawyer, a flashy uniform for the police officer, scrubs for the nurse and the surgeon, a T-shirt and jeans for the student, and rain gear for the fisherman (my grandfather was a fisherman in Newfoundland). But they are all working in the marketplace. In this book I am defining *marketplace* not narrowly as business enterprise but all human enterprise where exchange takes place, where ideas are shared, where human energy is expressed in creativity and innovation—which certainly includes homemaking, pastoring, delivering goods, and producing products. It includes musicians and artists and garbage collectors. I still work, by the way, even though I will be eighty-four by the time this book is published. I work not just in writing and teaching but serving in the Institute for Marketplace Transformation. But why write about the marketplace and the reign of God? Why put these two things together? Here is my answer: because the kingdom of God is right there in the workplace and can be announced and implemented there.

The New World Coming

Getting off an airplane one day, I noticed the very engaging advertisements in the Jetway placed there by a global bank expressing where this bank saw things were heading in the world—all under the title, "There is a new world coming." That's it, I thought. That's the central message of Jesus. It is the heart of the good news, the *godspel* (good tale in old English) which, according to Jesus is this: the kingdom of God has come and is coming. There is indeed a new world coming.

The first message of Jesus was "Repent for the kingdom of God is within your grasp" (Matt 4:17, N. T. Wright's translation). Jesus' last message on earth, before his ascension, was on the kingdom (Acts 1:3). By my calculation Jesus spoke about the kingdom of God 129 times and only three times about the church in the Gospel accounts. It is the master thought of Jesus, the key to grasping what Christianity is all about, and the genesis of the hope we have for our own daily work in this struggling world. Andy Crouch in *Culture Making* puts the ministry of Jesus clearly in kingdom terms: "His good news foretold a comprehensive restructuring of social life comparable to that experienced by a people when one monarch was succeeded by another. The Kingdom of God would touch every sphere and every scale of culture. . . . It would reshape . . . integrity in business and honesty in prayer."[1]

We begin to experience this new world coming right now. But the full renewal of everything will be completed when the end has come and when Christ comes a second time (Matt 19:28; Rev 21:5). The Christian gospel is not just getting our souls saved and gaining a ticket to enter heaven when we die. Yes, that is part of it. Remarkably, the former Pope Benedict XVI, Joseph Ratzinger, commented on this truncated good news in his book *What It Means to Be a Christian* (2006): "Christian theology . . . in the course of time turned the kingdom of God into a kingdom of heaven that is beyond this mortal life; the well-being of men became a salvation of souls, which again comes to pass beyond this life, after death." This tendency of spiritualization, Ratzinger said, is not the message of Jesus Christ.[2] So the whole gospel is for the whole of life and the whole of creation with deep integration and profound renewal including our work, workers, and workplaces. But if the kingdom is for now, how do we enter it?

Entering the Beauty and the Pain of the Kingdom

"Very truly I tell you, no one can see the kingdom of God
unless they are born again."

—JESUS, JOHN 3:3

The beauty of the kingdom is the world "set to rights," as N. T. Wright is fond of saying. It is life as it was meant to be. But there is not only beauty in the kingdom but pain in entering it. We enter the kingdom of God by repentance, a turning from self to God and his rule (Matt 3:2; 4:17). We do this by hearing and responding to the good news that God's rule in Jesus

1. Cited in Witherington, *Work*, 116.
2. Benedict XVI, *What It Means to Be a Christian*.

has been brought near to us, is within our grasp. That involves turning from self and this-age life to Jesus wholeheartedly. In doing this we renounce our own righteousness and in humility and childlikeness, come to the King. But behind our response to the kingdom is the call and initiative of God. Paul said, "[God] calls you into his kingdom and glory" (1 Thess 2:12), a call that goes out to everyone. Our response is to seek primarily the kingdom, to desire God and God's rule in Jesus, to seek the kingdom of God as a first priority in life (Matt 6:33).

We enter the kingdom through humility and childlikeness (Matt 18:3)—humble dependence. So, says Jesus, the kingdom belongs to children (Matt 19:14) and the childlike. To these, he said, "[My] Father has been pleased to give you the kingdom" (Luke 12:32). Indeed, many who talk about the kingdom but do not conform to the will of the Father and do not depend on him, will not enter the kingdom (Matt 7:21–23). It is those who actually do the Father's will who know the Lord and are in association or communion with him who will enter the kingdom. The terrifying words of Jesus in Matthew 7:23, "I never knew you," are reserved for people that have no relationship with Jesus even though they have done good works. Ironically, many outsiders will enter the kingdom and will feast with Abraham, Isaac, and Jacob, while those who were supposed to be in the kingdom will themselves be outsiders (Matt 8:11–12). Prostitutes and tax collectors enter before "righteous" people because they repent (Matt 21:31–32). So behind the entrance question is the issue of worthiness.

Our righteousness, said Jesus, must exceed that of the scribes and Pharisees for us to enter the kingdom (Matt 5:20). This means that our worthiness is not in religious performance or good works but in wholehearted trust in the King himself and the world that is coming. Through his death and resurrection Christ imputes his righteousness to us. Martin Luther called this a double exchange: our sin to Jesus (on the cross) and his righteousness attributed to us through our faith. To experience this brings about redemption of our persons and the forgiveness of sins.

Paul writes, "He has rescued us from the dominion of darkness and brought us into the kingdom of the Son he loves, in whom we have redemption" (Col 1:13–14). In reality this is not easy. It is not "cheap grace." It involves suffering as we are torn away from life lived only for this age ("in the flesh") to life in the Spirit and for the age to come. So Paul preached that we must go through many hardships to enter the kingdom of God (Acts

14:22). But it is suffering blended with joy. It is a mystery but a mystery revealed, long hidden from the eyes of humankind but now made plain.[3]

So why write about the kingdom of God when there are so many books on the church, on the individual's life in the Spirit, and so many how-to books on the pragmatics of following Jesus?

The Kingdom Perspective

There are two reasons for this book. First, the kingdom is the missing dimension in most presentations of the gospel and the marketplace. And yet it occupied Jesus fully. The kingdom is the integrating theme of the entire Bible (see chapters 4, 5, and 6 on this). From the beginning God intended to exercise his sovereignty through his entire creation and commissioned his God-imaging creature (humankind) to flesh out God's purpose in all of life and all of creation, in other words to bring in the kingdom. Those seminal passages in Genesis 1:28 and 2:15—"fill the earth and subdue it . . . rule . . . work it and take care of it"—are God saying, in effect, work with me and in harmony with my purposes in bringing in the kingdom, developing the potential of creation, and bringing human flourishing everywhere. But there is a second reason why I am taking a kingdom approach to the marketplace.

The kingdom of God is holistic, concerning all of the human person (not just the soul), the whole of human life in the world and all of creation, including the work, worker, and the workplace. Sin disrupted the program. But grace has largely restored God's intention of bringing full-orbed transformation. To do this God called a family and then a nation to embody his rule in a spiritual-social-political reality that involved a winsome lifestyle that would make Israel a light to the nations. But with the New Testament we enter a new phase of kingdom coming. The King has come in working clothes, born in a working-class, blue-collar home, and himself a tradesperson.

Jesus was counter religious-cultural in a double way. He was an enigma to those around him. For example, after Jesus turned five loaves and two small fish into enough food to feed five thousand people, the crowd wanted to take him by force and make him king (John 6:15). But he knew that in

---

3. George Eldon Ladd explains the mystery of the kingdom this way: "The kingdom of God is here but not with irresistible power. The kingdom has come, but it is not like a stone grinding an image to powder. On the contrary, it is like a man sowing seed. It does not force itself upon men." Ladd, *Gospel of the Kingdom*, 56.

their hearts they wanted a king who would eliminate the Romans from their cherished promised land by force, using what Luther called right-handed power, brute force—you-better-knuckle-down force. Much later there is a fascinating interchange when he was being tried by Pilate. The Roman governor, Pilate, asks Jesus, "Are you the king of the Jews?" (John 18:33). Jesus responds by saying, "My kingdom is not of this world. . . . My kingdom is from another place" (18:36). "You are a king, then!" said Pilate (18:37). And Jesus answers enigmatically, saying in effect, I am, but not the kind of king you are thinking about. Ironically, Pilate fastened a notice to be placed over his cross that said, "Jesus of Nazareth, the king of the Jews." In passing we may note that to call Jesus King is the same as to call him Lord, or Lord of lords, or Messiah, something eventually everyone will do (Phil 2:11). So what kind of king is he? His ministry was boundary-breaking, reaching out to the poor, the lost, the rejected, the prostitute, and the tax extortioner. He was countercultural. Why? As my pastor put it in his Palm Sunday address reflecting on Jesus entering Jerusalem on a young donkey: "*because his focus was never about the church but the kingdom.*"[4] But for now we must ask what the kingdom has to do with the workplace.

The Marketplace Perspective

Wai Yen Millie Chan is a Malaysian lawyer and a board member of the Institute for Marketplace Transformation. Listen to her heart as she recounts her experience of the marketplace:

> The marketplace is a rugged landscape steeped in entrenched organizational cultures (chiefly profit-centred), unfair and dehumanizing practices and expectations, injustice, and corruption. Nevertheless, I started my legal practice (then not a Christian) with a positive view (uncritically and unconsciously) of work, deeply influenced by my father's perspective that work flourishes the community, and every paycheck feeds not just the employee, but also the family.

Millie continues by relating what happened when she entered the kingdom and met the King.

---

4. Interim Pastor Tom Mei, Palm Sunday notes, West Point Grey Baptist Church, Vancouver, BC, March 28, 2021, emphasis mine.

When I accepted Christ in my early 40's, the floodgate opened with torrents of questions about life in Christ—with workplace issues often taking centre stage. Yet I do not recall a single sermon concerning work in the marketplace. As I struggled between old and new thinking, there were occasions I felt that working life might be easier for non-Christians. I was also under the impression that my colleagues who had grown up in Christian homes were better equipped to deal with marketplace challenges. This proves to be a misconception. Even now when I mention to second and third generation Christians about the mission of The Institute for Marketplace Transformation (IMT) in helping Christians to integrate faith with work, many express incredulity that the Bible actually teaches about these issues. Some maintain a conviction that our faith should be placed on silent mode when entering the workplace, while others share a profound sense of despondence that workplace problems are too monumental to solve.[5]

All good human enterprise is kingdom work. Kingdom work is not secular work and it is not religious work. It is work that advances the government of God, the rule of God, and makes people thrive. So the marketplace is one of the arenas where we can see the kingdom, where we can serve the kingdom, where we can be a sacramental presence for the kingdom.

Eight founding principles of the Institute for Marketplace Transformation[6] have originated over many decades of study, service, and discussion:

1. Service in the marketplace, through providing goods and services, through building an organizational culture and community, through relationships with co-workers, clients, and customers, is part of God's intended kingdom work to be done in the world.

2. Just as Jesus spoke, ministered, and located himself primarily in the marketplace, the primary location in which the mission of God today is to be implemented is the local and global marketplace.

3. Business, whether for-profit or not-for-profit, is a morally serious calling with implicit moral demands requiring trust and integrity, salty values in the kingdom of God.

4. There is no location in society that is so demonized and so debased that a Christian might not be called to serve there. The kingdom is

---

5. Wai Yen Millie Chan, Guided Study paper for Regent College, April 2021, unpublished, with permission from the author.

6. Imtglobal.org.

sown into the world with good mixed in with the bad. See the parable of the Weeds in Matthew 13:24–30.

5. The mission of Christians in the marketplace is not only to announce the good news of the kingdom of God (*kergyma*) but to build community (*koinonia*), to provide services (*diakonia*), and to work for justice and righteousness (the prophetic role).

6. Working in the marketplace can be an arena of spiritual growth and work itself in the kingdom of God is a spiritual discipline leading us into further maturity.

7. Working and ministering in the marketplace involves engaging principalities and powers, "the world, the flesh, and the devil." These powers must be addressed (and grappled with) through a variety of means: prayer, suffering powerlessness, incarnational engagement, and the censure of personal and structural sin.

8. As a kingdom mission IMT embraces the complexity of the here, and not here, [the] having come and coming of the rule of God. This means that IMT, along with Jesus, embraces a holistic, integral mission that includes the transformation of persons, taking care of human needs, engaging the powers and the stewardship of Creation.

The Book in Brief

So in this study we will examine from Scripture what is the kingdom, especially as it relates to our work in the world. First we start with images of the kingdom in the marketplace: metaphors and dimensions of human flourishing used by Jesus, drawing on his inaugural sermon in his home synagogue and his later teaching. We will meet people in the Bible like Rahab, who was a double agent for the kingdom while she lived and worked in the world as is (chapters 1 to 3). Then, second, we move to the important question of how the kingdom comes, whether it is entirely the work of God (this is a biblical survey from Genesis to Revelation), or whether we have some part cooperating as co-creators with God. We will explore a pithy saying of the apostle Paul from Colossians about the King in working clothes, though the term is not actually used (chapters 4 to 6). Third, we attend to the values and virtues of the kingdom in Scripture, the mystery of the kingdom, primarily its timing (chapters 7 and 8).

Fourth, we explore serving in the kingdom and the marketplace through ministry, mission, and leadership in the kingdom (chapters 9, 10, and 11). We consider how and why we can grow spiritually in the kingdom and the marketplace as we consider spiritual growth through actually giving leadership. Fifth, we deal with spiritual resistance to the kingdom in the marketplace, with the church and its relationship to the kingdom, ending with the empowering vision of the kingdom fully come in the new heaven and new earth. Here we will ask whether any of our work in this life will last, as well as whether we will work in heaven (chapters 12 to 14).

***

My friend and colleague Charles Ringma puts it this way: "The kingdom of God is all of God's upholding, renewing, and fulfilling activity in the world and we are invited to participate in this, witness to it, and rejoice in its manifestations."[7] So read on. I hope you will find it a great adventure.

---

7. Ringma, email, February 8, 2021.

PART ONE

Images of the Kingdom in the Marketplace

1

Kingdom Flourishing
in the Marketplace

"The most striking feature of contemporary culture is the unslaked craving
for transcendence."

—Andrew Delbanco[1]

"The proclamation of both the Jewish and Christian Scriptures is that the
God of Abraham, Isaac, Jacob, and (Father of) Jesus Christ offers the only
true, full, and enduring human flourishing available in the world."

—Jonathan T. Pennington[2]

My wife, Gail, leaned over the lunch table and said, "Please get the fertil-
izer out. Our indoor flowers are just surviving and they need to flourish."
That is what the kingdom of God is about—not just flowers, of course, but
people and places. Flourishing is exactly what the kingdom of God, that
great good news announced and embodied in Jesus, brings about—life on
steroids in contrast to just surviving.

The kingdom of God is all about this new way of being human in
the world and forever. In Luke's Gospel, Jesus' return to his hometown and
home synagogue comes right after the temptation narratives. So it is very

1. Quoted in Pink, *Whole New Mind*, 35.
2. Pennington, *Sermon on the Mount and Human Flourishing*, 290–91.

early in his ministry. He grew up in Nazareth, a flea-bitten little town about which people used to say, "Can anything good come out of Nazareth?" He has done some teaching and healings in Capernaum and some rumors drifted back to the old neighbors and his family. Jesus goes back to his home church. I know what that is like. It is scary.

Jesus in His Home Church

I grew up in a very large church in Toronto, Canada, a very formal church, so formal that the ushers wore tuxedos. The pastors wore academic gowns and hoods. Everyone was well-dressed and coiffed. People arrived in their Packards, the equivalent to a Lexus or Jaguar today. A few even came in chauffeured vehicles. We had a huge pipe organ that could almost wake the dead. We had four paid soloists. I was a teenager in that church and people remembered me as a teenager (and all that that means). But late in my teens I came to know Jesus and was the first person in a very long time in that church to do theological studies and to become a pastor. After many, many years I was invited back to speak. I know what it is like! The feeling.

The text read that Saturday in Nazareth was Isaiah 61:1–7.

> The Spirit of the Sovereign Lord is on me, because the Lord has anointed me to proclaim good news to the poor. He has sent me to bind up the brokenhearted. To proclaim freedom for the captives and release from darkness for the prisoners, to proclaim the year of the Lord's favor . . . (Isa 61:1–2).

After the whole passage was read Jesus simply said, "Today this scripture is fulfilled in your hearing" (Luke 4:21). He said, in effect, "This is what I came to do. I am come that they may have life and have it to the full" (or abundantly, John 10:10).

People were in awe. The passage points to God's special messenger, God's Messiah or Anointed One, who would bring salvation and renewal. The term *Messiah* was used about the King and the kingdom. The passage also suggests that the wonderful prophecy in Leviticus 25 about the year of Jubilee had really come. Slaves would be set free, land would be restored to the original owners, and people would flourish—all of this embodied in the life and work of a hometown boy from Nazareth. Why is this important?

From Genesis to Revelation, the Bible is about the kingdom of God. Robert Farrar Capon says the Bible is primarily about the "mystery of the kingdom" and a mystery "by definition is something well hidden and not at all likely to be grasped by plausibility-loving minds."[3] And he continues to argue that the Bible is "about the mystery by which the power of God works to form this world into the Holy City, the New Jerusalem that comes down from heaven from God, prepared as a bride adorned for her husband."[4] Here is a hometown boy saying, in effect, the kingdom has come in me! Speaking about the title put over Jesus on the cross, "The king of the Jews," Oscar Cullman, a Swiss theologian, regards the inscription as "almost certain proof that Jesus in some way made himself the subject of his preaching on the kingdom of God soon to come."[5]

In a deep article by Chrys C. D. Caragounis, a Swedish professor, it is noted that Jesus' conception of the kingdom of God was dynamic—not just a territory of land, but the active and renewing influence of God as King. He carefully shows how Jesus' view was in continuity with the Old Testament promise and even had some shared features with the apocalyptic kingdom that would appear at the end of time, but "went beyond them in certain important respects":

1. The kingdom of God was primarily dynamic rather than a geographical entity;

2. it was connected with the destiny of the Son of man [the preferred self-designation of Jesus];

3. entrance into it would not be based on the covenant or confined to Jewish participation and

4. whereas in apocalypticism it was a vague future hope, in Jesus it is definite and imminent; in fact it demands immediate response.[6]

So at the beginning of his ministry Jesus is announcing what the kingdom brings: life to the full—at least partly now and fully at the end of history when Christ returns, restoring maximum human life and a completely renewed creation. It has many aspects.

3. Capon, *Parables of the Kingdom*, 5.

4. Capon, *Parables of the Kingdom*, 15.

5. Quoted in Klappert, "King," 379.

6. Caragounis, "Kingdom of God/Heaven," 420. This extensive article reviews not only the New Testament references to the kingdom but the extensive theological literature on whether the kingdom had come, was coming at the end of history, or both.

Economic Flourishing

The first has to do with provision. The Spirit of the Lord, so the text says, is on the Messiah and anointed him to "proclaim good news to the poor" (Luke 4:18). The Hebrew word for "the poor" is *anawin*, which means the downtrodden and the disadvantaged, people held back from thriving either by circumstances or by other people. My wife and I have known and lived among many *anawin*. We have a friend in East Africa who is a single mom with three children. Her husband left her for another woman. She buys secondhand clothes in a major city and sells them in the local market. She struggles to get enough money to feed her family and pay their school fees. What does it mean for her to hear and experience good news?

Simply, it is this: that she has enough to thrive. It happened to the widow in Zarephath during a famine. The prophet Elijah was directed by God to visit her. During the meeting he asked her for bread and water. But all she had was a handful of flour and a little jug of olive oil. Then there was some good news. In Elijah's presence, "The jar of flour was not used up and the jug of oil did not run dry, in keeping with the word of the Lord spoken by Elijah" (1 Kgs 17:16). Yes, sometimes it is by a miracle. Sometimes this does require a handout in times of extreme crises—wars, famines, or plagues—but for the long haul it means a hand-up, providing the means by which people can thrive. The medieval Jew Maimonides (Moses ben Maimon, 1135–1204) defined charity's eight degrees by ranking them:

1. A person gives, but only when asked by the poor.

2. A person gives, but is glum when giving.

3. A person gives cheerfully, but less than he should.

4. A person gives without being asked, but gives directly to the poor. Now the poor know who gave them help and the giver, too, knows whom he has benefited.

5. A person throws money into the house of someone who is poor. The poor person does not know to whom he is indebted, but the donor knows whom he has helped.

6. A person gives his donation in a certain place and then turns his back so that he does not know which of the poor he has helped, but the poor person knows to whom he is indebted.

7. A person gives anonymously to a fund for the poor. Here the poor person does not know to whom he is indebted, and the donor does not know whom he has helped.

But the highest, says the Jewish rabbi, is this:

8. Money is given to prevent another from becoming poor, such as providing him with a job or by teaching him a trade or by setting him up in business and not be forced to the dreadful alternative of holding out his hand for charity. This is the highest step and the summit of charity's golden ladder.[7]

In the kingdom of God people will help people, even economically as we have seen, in micro- and mid-sized economical development. So, in this matter, "our limbs become the limbs and organs of the Holy Spirit," said early church father John Chrysostom.[8] But sometimes the need for renewal is not outside but inside.

Emotional Flourishing

In the Greek version of Isaiah 61, the Messiah King, also the Servant, brings emotional flourishing. "He has sent me to bind up the brokenhearted" (Isa 61:1). There are so many ways to become brokenhearted: being rejected, having a precious relationship severed, or experiencing profound loss. But sometimes it is not what others have done to us but what we have done to ourselves—profound disappointment and grief over our own behavior so we are either experiencing emotional prostration or conviction of sin. Guilt is the feeling of having done something wrong. It can become all-consuming. Shame, the first emotion mentioned in the Bible, is even deeper than guilt and understood better in Asia than in the West. If guilt is "I have *done* something wrong," shame is "*I* am wrong." It is profoundly disabling. Let me visualize this for you.

In a hotel in Indonesia I saw a sculpture of a person experiencing shame. His head was buried in his legs, crunched down towards the floor like a closed, inwardly focused ball of flesh, unwilling to look up, incapable of releasing himself from his inwardness. But the kingdom deals with this. People say time heals everything. But it does not. What heals is love. And

---

7. Quoted in Diehl and Diehl, *It Ain't Over Till It's Over*, 129–30.

8. Quoted in Leech, *True Prayer*, 78.

God loves relentlessly, extravagantly, redemptively, binding up the broken heart, soothing and restoring to wholeness.[9] But some of the redemption includes being released from external bondage.

Personal Flourishing

When the prophet says on behalf of the Messiah that this Spirit-anointed one will "proclaim release to the captives," he is announcing the manumission of people from slavery—manumission is that great word used when slaves are made free. Here is the Year of Jubilee actually happening (Lev 25:10; Jer 34:8). During that year slaves were to be freed and all debts cancelled. All land, mortgaged or sold for the survival of the owners, was to be returned to the family. And here speaking in Nazareth is Jubilee embodied in Jesus. The kingdom is coming. Liberation can take place outside and inside. Outside forces can lead us into captivity: government powers, wars, and the transportation of Israel to Babylon. It happens when people are forcibly removed from their homeland, as Israel was, or as people are today forced into the sex trade. But not all slavery involves external physical captivity. Some slavery is internal, such as addiction to drugs, sex, power, gaming, racism, work, or meaninglessness. But there is freedom. The kingdom is coming. And more.

Mental Flourishing

Admittedly the next phrase Jesus quoted is translated in the Greek version of the Old Testament not as "release from darkness to the prisoners" (Hebrew) but "the recovery of sight to the blind" (Greek). The Hebrew word actually means "wide-opening to the [people that are] bound,"[10] which does suggest becoming wide-eyed or clear-eyed, something Jesus actually accomplished with some people by physically restoring their sight. In fact the kingdom

9. In his wonderful article on "Human Flourishing and the Bible," Jonathan T. Pennington notes that there are three Hebrew words that describe human flourishing: *shalom*, which means wholeness; *asherem*, which means the state of someone who is flourishing, "the flourishing of fertility, prosperity, and security that come from faithfulness to the Lord and wise living"; and *tamin*, a word usually translated as "holy" but, as Pennington says, "a close examination of the Bible's use of 'holy' reveals that it means to be whole and complete," 44–46.

10. Motyer, *Prophecy of Isaiah*, 500.

brings both *out*-sight—clarity of physical vision—and *in*sight—clarity in perception. But without either there is blindness, outer or inner. With regard to out-sight: Jesus opened the eyes of the blind as a potent sign of what the kingdom would do for all people (John 9). After healing the man born blind there is a dynamic interchange between Jesus and the investigating Pharisees because Jesus did this healing on the Sabbath day. Why did he do what was seen as work on the Sabbath? There were six other days Jesus could have used—which is the very point his critics were making, insisting that only a sinner could do this on the Sabbath. Then they asked the man himself, who said, "One thing I do know. I was blind but now I see" (9:25). At the conclusion of the interchange between the Lord and the critics, the Pharisees posed a question: "Are we blind too?" This engagement ended with a damning statement by Jesus to the Pharisees about spiritual blindness: "If you were blind, you would not be guilty of sin; but now that you claim to see, your guilt remains" (9:41). What needs healing in the Pharisees and in people today is not only out-sight but insight.

C. S. Lewis once said, "I believe in Christianity as I believe that the Sun has risen, not only because I see it but because by it I see everything else."[11] Clear, open-eyed insight means to see everything the way it really is, to see human beings as God-imaging creatures, to see the world the way it is as the creation of God, but now turned away from God, to see the kingdom of God folded like yeast into the dough of this life and this world. This is surely what the English poet William Blake meant when he spoke of seeing not *with* the eye but *through* it, thereby suggesting that if our perception were truly cleansed we would see everything the way it truly is—infinite. Blake was asked whether, when we look at the sun we see a disk of fire like a shilling. "O no, no," he said, "I see an innumerable company of the Heavenly Host crying, 'Holy, Holy, Holy, is the Lord God Almighty.'"[12] But flourishing concerns the spirit of the human person. And what the Spirit yearns for within us is true happiness in the favor of God.

Spiritual Flourishing

Happiness is a universal desire. It is a major concern of the ancient Greek philosophers. *Eudaimonia*, the Greek word for happiness, is found in

11. Quoted by Loren Wilkinson on Christmas, Whidbey Island, 1975.
12. Blake, "Vision of the Last Judgment," 1027.

Stoicism, Epicureanism, Neoplatonism, and Aristotelianism.[13] But flourishing in the kingdom differs from the idea of flourishing in the ancient Greek philosophers. While the search for human happiness is universal, and that search exists in all religions, the biblical perspective on human flourishing has four differences, according to Jonathan T. Pennington. First, there is a difference in the *values*—what is considered praiseworthy and virtuous; second, a difference in the *people* who may experience flourishing—not merely the educated, philosophers, and the rich, but everyone; third, a difference in *goals*—in that flourishing can only be experienced in relationship with the living God; and fourth, especially a difference in *means*—in that people receive something from "outside ourselves" through the work of the Holy Spirit.[14] So in contrast with the statement that you can *be* anything you want to be, N. T. Wright puts it this way: "What you will be is what you already are in Christ"—it is all about grace.[15] But Isaiah in the passage uses a special word for this, not happiness but "favor."

This, the prophet says, is "the year of the Lord's favor" (Isa 61:2). Significantly when Jesus quoted from Isaiah 61 he deliberately neglected the next phrase, "and the day of the vengeance of our God." The reason is this: Jesus came to save, not to judge.[16] But he will come again and there will be universal judgment. So Jesus saw this prophecy as half-fulfilled in his own first coming—to make people right with God—and to be finally fulfilled when he returns a second time. In all events, what good news this is: favor with God.

Finding favor in one's family of origin is often deeply troubling. One young man longing for the approval of his father said, "Dad, I am doing my very best"—to which the father said, "Your best is not good enough." But finding favor with God, finding profound acceptance with God, is even deeper. In Acts 9 the story of Saul's slavish adherence to the law and his rapacious and murderous onslaught against Christians—whom he saw as dangerous heretics—is a case in point. His pre-Christian life can be seen

13. Pennington, "Human Flourishing and the Bible," 40.

14. Pennington, "Human Flourishing and the Bible," 51–53.

15. Quoted in Pennington, "Human Flourishing and the Bible," 52.

16. Motyer puts it this way: "Thus he [Jesus] expressed his own understanding of his mission at that point, not to condemn the world but to save the world (John 3:17). He was also aware, however, of a coming day when he would execute the judgment committed to him (John 5:22–29). In other words, what Isaiah sees as a double-faceted ministry the Lord apportions respectively to his first and second comings, the work of the Servant and of the Anointed Conqueror." Motyer, *Prophecy of Isaiah*, 499–500.

as a search for God's favor. Until he met Jesus on the Damascus road he was a *driven* person trying to find acceptance with God on the basis of his religious works. But when he met Jesus he became a *called* person—same person, same personality, same energy, but now with a very different motivation and life purpose. Why? Because he had found favor with God and that solely and simply on the basis of the grace of God and the reconciling work of Jesus on the cross. Martin Luther called this the great exchange. In effect Paul (and we) could say "I exchanged Christ's righteousness for my sin and Christ exchanged my sin for his righteousness" (2 Cor 5:21). Thus favor is found. It is, as Billy Graham once said, "just as though I hadn't sinned." Surely this is the heart of flourishing: knowing you have found favor with God and having the witness, the hug of the Spirit in your heart that you belong as a daughter or son in God's family (Rom 8:15–16). But there are yet other dimensions.

Workplace Flourishing

"They will rebuild the ancient ruins and restore the places long devastated; they will renew the ruined cities that have been devastated for generations" (Isa 61:4). We will flourish in the kingdom of God in our work. That means that work will be redemptive—restoring things that have been broken or debased, and work will be worshipful. In a fascinating and unique book, Matthew Kaemingk and Corey B. Willson reconnect our work with liturgy, both within the corporate worship of the people of God and in the workplace itself.[17] This is totally in line with Romans 12:1–2, where we are exhorted, in view of God's mercy, to present our whole bodily life to God as spiritual worship, including our work. So reconnecting faith and work, now a global movement,[18] must include seeing our work as worship, as prophesied by Isaiah, in which the flourishing people are clothed in "a garment of praise" and these oak trees, as they are called, would be a "display of [God's] splendor" (Isa 61:3). But to whom is the "they" referring to as rebuilding the devastated ruins?

17. See Kaemingk and Wilson, *Work and Worship*.

18. Institute for Marketplace Transformation (IMT) is part of a global movement to integrate faith and work. IMT offers films, courses, seminars, and leadership training. See https://imtglobal.org. For a survey of the present situation in the faith and work movement see Johnson and Rundle, "Distinctives and Challenges of Business as Mission." They note that in 2003 there were twelve hundred organizations associated with the movement, with more coming.

"They" refers to the people brought together by the anointed one, people obliquely mentioned as the "strangers" [who] "will shepherd your flocks" and the "foreigners" [who] "will work your fields and vineyards." The Messiah will bring together people who normally would have nothing to do with each other. From the New Testament we learn that the wall separating Jews and Gentiles, and any other groups of people that have nothing to do with each other, has been broken down by the cross of Jesus, thus making peace (Eph 2:14–18). So now there is neither Jew nor Greek, male or female, bond or free because "you are all one in Christ Jesus" (Gal 3:28). To this Mar Ostathios says, "The theological foundation of a classless society is the classless Godhead himself as a classless Nuclear family."[19] And here is where Jesus got into trouble in his home church.

Jesus almost got killed for noting that the prophets Elijah and Elisha both were sent to people outside the Jewish community and brought flourishing to them, anticipating the rich diversity of people in the kingdom of God who form unity *through*, and not in spite of, diversity. This was so offensive that they took Jesus out to the brow of a hill and were about to toss him over, while he walked right through the angry crowd and escaped.

These once alienated people, now that the breakdown is mended, will work together to rebuild society. And they do this through their work. We can do this provisionally now in the marketplace. Is this also a picture of the new heaven and new earth, the kingdom fully come, when "the renewal of all things" (Matt 19:28) will be taking place? Perhaps all heaven is growth, healing, and renewal. And how do we function as people flourishing in the kingdom of God?

Ministerial Flourishing

"And you will be called priests of the Lord, you will be named ministers of our God" (Isa 61:6). The priesthood of all believers was not invented in the Protestant Reformation. It was already there in God's mandate for Israel, with the call to all Israel to be a royal priesthood (Exod 19:6). It is found here as well in the picture of Jubilee flourishing. It concerns not just the formal ministerial, but all the people. That means that everyone is in full-time ministry. Priests are bridge builders and just as most bridges have two-way traffic, it is so with the priestly people. They bring people and places to God in prayer and intercession; they bring God to people and places through

19. Quoted in Leech, *Experiencing God*, 379.

service and mission—two-way traffic. Worship and mission are the two sides of the priestly coin. They bear the presence of God in the everyday-ness of life and bring everyday life to God as a sacrament of thanksgiving.

Human flourishing is surely one of the most wonderful aspects of the coming of the kingdom, partly now and eventually completely. The flour-ishing is total: economic, emotional, personal, mental, spiritual, workplace, and ministerial. If this is not good news, then I cannot imagine what is! No wonder that the dominant mood of the passage in Isaiah 61 is joy, twice mentioned. Those who mourn for the present situation will receive "the oil of joy" and "everlasting joy will be yours" (61:3, 7). Joy is a divine infusion of exhilaration, the touch of God and the most distinctive experience of people in the kingdom of God.

So if the kingdom is so good why not live in it, for it, and work in it?

A Prayer

Gracious God, thank you that you do not want us merely to sur-vive but to flourish. You came in Jesus that we may have life and life to the full.

Lord, some of us need your touch, we hear you knocking at the door of our lives, your voice . . . and we open the door; please come in and have fellowship with us.

Some of us feel we are half-saved, half-healed, half-restored, half-renewed. . . . If it is your pleasure, please continue that won-derful and gracious work of renewal in us.

Thank you for giving us your favor, that we are accepted by you, blessed by you.

Thank you that you have called us to be priests even if we are wounded healers and not as whole as we would like, but will be when you come again. Amen.

2

On Being a Double Agent in the Marketplace

[The Christian] is the citizen of another kingdom, and it is thence
that he derives his way of thinking, judging and feeling. His heart
and his thought are elsewhere. He is the subject of another State. . . .
He may also be sent out as a spy.

—JACQUES ELLUL[1]

ONE FINDS SAINTS IN strange places. Jesus found them among prostitutes
and tax collectors! The Old Testament person Rahab is acknowledged in
the New Testament as a heroine of faith (Jas 2:25; Heb 11:31). She was a
prostitute but acted like a double agent spy. This curious character from the
book of Joshua may have also used her home as an inn. But she certainly
had kingdom shrewdness. Jesus was later to say, "Be as shrewd as snakes
and as innocent as doves" (Matt 10:16), something which was shown by the
two spies sent by Joshua to spy out the land they were to possess, as well
as by Rahab herself. Rahab lived in a house either on top of the wall or in
the wall of the ancient city of Jericho, on the edge of Israel's promised land
(Josh 2:1–24). Why would the spies choose to go to the home of a prostitute? Certainly they would be safe there and who would know better what
was really going on in the land than she, much like the hairdresser or barber
who serves most of the women and men in a community! And Rahab knew

1. Ellul, *Presence of the Kingdom*, 45.

24

that the people were melting in fear of the Israelites. This was in the period when, after a whole generation of wandering in the wilderness, the people of Israel were about to possess the land promised to them. Two spies were sent in to snoop out what the country was like, how difficult it would be to possess it, what kind of opposition they would face, and where the defences were weakest. But it was not the first time spies were sent in.

Spying for the Kingdom

A generation earlier twelve spies were sent into the promised land and came back to the people with a bad report. The people there, they said, were giants. The spies felt like grasshoppers in comparison. Israel would be smeared. All quivered in fear—all, that is, except two spies who said that with God's help they could defeat the inhabitants of the promised land (Num 13). But the other ten, with their bad report, tried to convince the people living in the desert to return to Egypt for safety. All these people died in the desert, except Joshua, aide to Moses. Now a generation later there is a second spying operation, with two spies this time. This is where Rahab comes in.

Why am I telling you this story? Because it is a parable of what it is like to live and work in the world and yet to belong to the kingdom of God. We are double agents serving two kingdoms[2] at the same time. A contemporary French philosopher and theologian, Jacques Ellul, suggested this model of the kingdom person, living and working in one kingdom but spying out the actual indications and potential of another kingdom that eventually will take over completely.

> In fact that is the situation of the Christian: to work in secret, at the heart of the world, for his Lord; to prepare for his Lord's victory from within; to create a nucleus in this world, and to discover its secrets, in order that the kingdom of God may break forth in splendor.[3]

---

2. A very developed treatment of Martin Luther's "Two Kingdoms" involves accepting the reality of the kingdom of God and the kingdom of the world. In this Luther draws a line between spiritual authority and temporal authority, based on the New Testament teaching of the two ages, the old age and the new age (of the Spirit). See Nygren, "Luther's Doctrine of the Two Kingdoms."

3. Ellul, *Presence of the Kingdom*, 45.

Rahab was a Canaanite, a citizen of her own country. She was a businessperson. She received two Israelite spies in her home and embraced faith in the King of kings, Yahweh. As one commentator says, "That the two men had entered her house with honorable intentions may have contributed to this decision, for their conduct too must have filled her with respect for Israel's God."[4] But when she saw the thousands of Israelites in the desert on the edge of the promised land, when she realized that God was in this, when she heard what God had done even forty years previously in splitting the Red Sea, and what God did with the kings of Sihon and Og on the way to the promised land, she hid the spies and said, "The Lord your God is God of heaven above and earth below" (Josh 2:11). Simply, she embraced the kingdom of God and threw her lot in with the spies. The king of Jericho heard that the Hebrew spies were in Rahab's house and demanded that she bring them out. Here is where she demonstrates faith-filled shrewdness.

Rahab's Shrewd Behavior

Rahab hid the men on the roof under raw flax stalks and protected them. Then when the king's men came and inquired about the Israelite spies, she diverted them: "I did not know where they had come from . . . At dusk they left . . . I don't know which way they went. Go after them quickly. You may catch up with them" (2:4–5)—which is what the king's men did. Did she do wrong or right in diverting the king's men with a lie or a deliberate evasion?[5] Now while these Canaanites were scooting off to the Jordan fords to try to catch them, Rahab went up on the roof and confessed to the two spies using the word, Yahweh, that connotes that God is the God of Israel, "I know that the Lord has given you this land and that a great fear of you has fallen on us" (2:9). She shrewdly uses covenant language, for she is a believer and asks for a clear sign that they, for their part, will "show kindness [the Hebrew word, *hesed*, for the glue of the covenant—love and faithfulness] to my family, because I have shown kindness [again *hesed*] to you" (2:12). "Our lives for your lives!," the Hebrew spies responded. They, for their part,

---

4. Goslinga, *Joshua, Judges, Ruth*, 46.

5. We see the same shrewdness in the Hebrew midwives in Egypt when they were commanded by Pharaoh to kill all the Hebrew baby boys. "Hebrew women are not like Egyptian women; they are vigorous and give birth before the midwives arrive" (Exod 1:19). The text says "because the Hebrew midwives feared God [more than Pharaoh], he gave them families of their own" (1:21). Thus Moses was saved.

would fulfill their part of the agreement provided that Rahab would not tell to anyone what they were doing. Then she lowered the two men down from the wall on a rope and suggested that the Hebrew spies should hide in the hills for three days, after which they could return to Joshua, which is what they did. But the agreement had conditions.

She must gather her family into her home, and let down a scarlet rope as a sign to the invading Israelites. So "she tied the scarlet cord in the window" (2:21), possibly wound up to be ready for the great day of her rescue. And indeed when the Israelite thousands captured Jericho and saw the rope lowered, she and her family were saved. She now belonged to God's kingdom and to God, making a clean break from her Canaanite gods.

But who saved whom?

Rahab was saved by Israel but she also saved Israel. As a person of faith she had a comprehensive worldview. She admitted that the God of Israel was the center of everything. She could see the beginning of the union of heaven and earth, in other words, the kingdom of God. She embraced her citizenship in heaven (Phil 3:20). She had kingdom consciousness.

It is intriguing to consider that while the Israelite spies had a single identity, belonging only to the God-destined community, Rahab had a double identity, belonging both to the old age and the new age at the same time. So in a sense she is a better model of the Christian in the world today than even the two Hebrew spies, who belonged totally to the new age.

And the critical thing for today's Christian living and working in the world is the kingdom of God, God's new world coming. What does it do for us to see the reality of the kingdom for work, workers, and workplaces? What is it like to live and work with kingdom consciousness?

Kingdom Consciousness in the Workplace

We will, like Rahab, look for signs and indications that heaven and earth have come together. Let's take some examples of the kingdom from the last chapter and from people and places known to me, though their names have been changed. First, the kingdom means *good news for the poor*. I have just received an email from Ron, who has raised money to assist people he knows in a theological seminary in the majority world, who have had their salaries slashed during the pandemic and are buying oxygen tanks and tents for people affected, since the hospitals cannot take them. Their work is the kingdom coming. Second, the kingdom means *emotional flourishing*. Two dear friends started an enterprise together but they experienced a major roadblock in their relationship, leading to one blasting the other with words he did not even know were in his heart, to his own utter surprise and to the chagrin of the other, who resigned and got out of the enterprise altogether. Both were brokenhearted. But, by the grace of God they were ultimately reconciled and their broken hearts were healed. (I know this story is true because I am the one who blasted the other.) That is the kingdom coming. Third, the kingdom means *personal flourishing*: "release to the captives." Joan is addicted to alcohol and unable to hold down her job, even as her husband sometimes covers for her, unintentionally enabling her addiction. But then, by the grace of God and through AA, she is delivered and is gainfully employed and flourishing. That is the kingdom coming.

Fourth, the kingdom means *mental flourishing* as the eyes of the blind—both in out-sight and insight—are opened. Jacob, a Christian judge in the United States, faithfully undertook his justice work for decades without seeing that what he was doing was loving God and neighbor through his work, as well as bringing in the kingdom. Through a seminar he began to see his daily work as a ministry. He praised God and his heart sang as he went to work. "If only I had known this thirty years ago when I started. And yet, with what joy I now work," he exclaimed. That is the kingdom coming.

Fifth, the kingdom means *spiritual flourishing*: "the year of the Lord's favour." James, a PhD student at the local university, phoned in the early hours of Monday morning. "I was in church with you last night and heard you speak. You answered all my questions about becoming a Christian except one." This led to an extensive weekly conversation and to this choice person becoming a follower of Jesus, returning to his country to lead a vast organization in his home country where he remains to this day as a leader. That is the kingdom coming.

Sixth, the kingdom means *workplace flourishing*: "they will restore the places long devastated." Chun Wei, a young medical intern, sits on the bed of an AIDS patient at a time when the only hospital in the city that will take people afflicted with HIV was a Roman Catholic hospital. She explains that there will be a resurrection of our bodies. That is the kingdom coming. Sandra, a mom, creates a family environment in which the children can thrive, attending to the environment of the home, the meals and the conversations. That is the kingdom coming. Frank, a theological seminary grad who took over his father's retail automotive business, has crafted a business that is truly a kingdom business in its organizational culture, management style, empowerment of employees, and customer service. "I want to run a business that brings glory to God," Frank says. That is the kingdom coming.

Seventh, the kingdom means *ministerial flourishing*: "you will be called priests of the Lord." Jim is a person with a pastoral heart. But to the surprise of his boss he turns down a promotion into management in IBM because "what I have to give to this company is my care of people." Eventually he retires from IBM and begins to spend all his time hanging around the bicycle couriers in the city, loving them and listening to them. When, through age and ill health, he is forced to move closer to his family in another city, these men and women bicycle couriers come in the hundreds to a celebratory and thanksgiving event. That is the kingdom coming.

The thing about all these signs of the kingdom is this: they are found in normal life, not just in religious life. The kingdom means that the line between sacred and secular is erased.[6] All things are within the sphere of God's sovereignty.[7] (We will deal with the pernicious effect of dualism in chapter 7.) Gone is the idea that if you are really serious about following Jesus you will become a pastor or missionary. Kingdom work is not secular work. So when people say to me, "I am leaving secular work and going into the Lord's work," I usually say, "But what were you doing before? It was the Lord's work. Of course, if God leads you from one kind of Lord's work to another kind of Lord's work, that is fine. But don't say you are now going 'full time' because there is no part-time option for followers of Jesus." But if kingdom work is not secular work, neither is it religious work. Jesus had most of his trouble from religious people. Kingdom work is good work that seeks to actually advance the kingdom of God in this world and in people.

All good work is doing kingdom work. Watering the flowers, preaching a sermon, making a deal or a meal, all can be done with kingdom consciousness, serving God and neighbor. My friend Steve Garber says we have a natural predisposition to dualism—to see some things as holy and other things as secular. What the good news of the kingdom of God does for us is this: it enables us to live and work seamlessly, all for God, all holy, all kingdom service, whether frying a hamburger as hamburgers were meant to be, or talking to a stranger about the new world coming and having come in Jesus. Rahab was conscious of the kingdom in the coming of the Israelites

6. For a development of how dualism emerged and how Scripture demolishes it, see Stevens and Lim, *Money Matters*, chapter 4, "God and Caesar."

7. The Barmen Declaration (1934) states: "We repudiate the false teaching that there are areas of life in which we belong not to Jesus Christ but [to] another lord." Leith, ed., *Creeds of the Churches*, 520.

into Canaan, and the God who was leading them. But it is not without hope of something even better. It is also not without problems. We need to be conscious that there is an anti-kingdom in the world. With kingdom consciousness we will experience difficulty, resistance, and trouble because we are embracing the kingdom and the King.

Anti-Kingdom Consciousness in the Workplace

In Acts 14:22, Paul and Barnabas, returning to the cities where they had planted churches—Lystra, Iconium and Antioch—said, "We must go through many hardships to enter the kingdom of God." So we will live and work counterculturally, as Rahab came to do. We wrestle not just with sinful people but with the principalities and powers. Jesus did, and got a reaction. Donald Kraybill describes the towel-and-basin service of Jesus (John 13):

> Jesus rankled the rich who oppressed the poor. He healed and shelled grain on the Sabbath. He ate with sinners and accepted tax collectors. He committed blasphemy, by calling God his *abba*, his daddy, and forgiving sins without sacrifice. He violated and condemned the oral law. He welcomed a prostitute's anointing touch. He travelled with women in public. His parables stung religious leaders. He talked freely with Samaritans and Gentiles. He healed the sick. He blessed the helpless. He touched lepers. He entered pagan homes. He purged the sacred temple. He stirred up large crowds. This was the Jesus movement in action. These acts, these politics of the basin, led directly to the cross.[8]

In due course chapter 12 will deal with the presence of the anti-kingdom, with grappling with the principalities and the powers, with wrestling with the world, the flesh, and the devil. But suffice it to say here that Jesus, speaking to his disciples, says ,"Whoever wants to be my disciple must deny themselves and take up their cross and follow me. For whoever wants to save their life will lose it, but whoever loses their life for me will find it" (Matt 16:24–5). I have brooded on this text for all of my life and have come to some conclusions.

Jesus is not talking about our disabilities, or diseases, or things over which we have no control. We are called to "*take up* our cross," not merely endure it. Living as a spy is a risky business. Contrary to what most people think, this "taking up your cross" does not mean simply submitting to life's

8. Kraybill, *Upside-Down Kingdom*, 245.

vicissitudes: a bad job, a difficult spouse, a problem child, a disease. "That is my cross," people say, but it isn't. So what does it mean? It means two things.

First, it means embracing what Jesus has done on the cross as sufficient for us and identifying ourselves with the finished work of Jesus. "Were you there when they crucified my Lord?" goes the old spiritual song. Yes, there goes me. "God made him who had no sin to be sin for us, so that in him we might become the righteousness of God" (2 Cor 5:21). Luther called this a double imputation. My sin was imputed to him. His righteousness was imputed to me. Lose your life and you will find it, Jesus said; find your life (autonomously) and you will lose it. If there is no passion in your heart for the Savior, you are dead. And yet ironically, Paul says, "We who are alive are always being given over to death for Jesus' sake, so that his life may be revealed in our mortal body" (2 Cor 4:11) and "I have been crucified with Christ" (Gal 2:20). Here is the ironic "I, yet not I." I no longer live. Christ lives in me.

So this agreement with the death and resurrection of Christ makes us, as the early Fathers said, more human. And ultimately our final death and resurrection makes us *perfectly* human.

But more deeply still, and second, taking up our own cross is not only having passion for the Savior but means *sharing the passion of Christ*. Paul himself spoke of filling up "what is still lacking in regard to Christ's afflictions" (Col 1:24). Paul, writing these words in prison for the gospel of the kingdom, meant this about his own suffering on behalf of others, especially the people of God, as though there was something more that is needed than simply thanking Christ, as we do in Communion, for his sacrifice. Our passion in Jesus is that we ourselves are to live and work sacrificially, sharing the passion of Jesus. Andrew Murray argued, "Jesus has many lovers of his cross but few who bear it. Many who follow him in drinking the communion cup, but few who will drink the cup he drank."[9] And how do we do that? We do this by entering into the experience of the cross. It is *our* cross but carried in fellowship with Jesus. We do this by engaging the suffering of the world, by entering into the affliction of the church, and by experiencing the pain of other people. In so doing we enter into and share the redemptive suffering of Jesus for people, for families, for nations, for the world, and for the marketplace. So, as Luther once said, there is a cross to be taken up in the marketplace.

---

9. Murray, *Like Christ*, 56–57.

Someone said that unlike Buddhism, which finds a supernatural *cure* for suffering, Christianity finds a supernatural *use* for suffering through living into the cross and resurrection of Jesus. At the communion table we enter into the redemptive, successful, and transformative suffering of Jesus. We don't just chew bread and drink grape juice or wine. We ingest Jesus into our hearts. We eat him up. We take up our cross. We embrace a cruciform life. And we do this not only in the sacrament of the table but in the sacrament of everyday life—in work, relationships, friendship, hostility, and rejection. We embrace Jesus through his cross and resurrection, and we experience a little of what he did. This is what it means to be a double agent spy, living and working in the present reality but at the same time living and working for the kingdom of God. Like Rahab.

The pastor who officiated at our wedding used to run a Saturday night coffee shop in the basement of the church in Glasgow, Scotland. One night he spoke at length with a prostitute. Her whole dark and dirty story was unraveled. At the end of the evening he arranged for someone to drive her home, as much of a home as she would have. For his part he went home feeling dirty. Even after a shower he still felt dirty. He slept fitfully through the night and woke up still feeling the weight of her life—dirty. In contrast, on the way to her home, the prostitute said to the gentleman who drove her home, "Talking to that man made me feel clean." The pastor said of the experience, "I think I experienced a little of what Jesus did on the cross."

So in kingdom consciousness we will live and work counterculturally but within the culture, like Rahab. Jesus said it cryptically, aptly, and provocatively in the Gospel of John: we are to work *in* the world but not to be *of* the world. Indeed he is praying that we will not be taken *out* of the world (John 17:15–16), the very thing many Christians are trying to achieve. But there is also joy in the kingdom, to which subject we now turn.

3

So, What Is It like on the Inside?

"In the Bible shalom means *universal flourishing, wholeness and delight.*"

—Cornelius Plantinga Jr.[1]

"We demand to experience the evidence."

—R. D. Laing[2]

Years ago I was involved on the university campuses of eastern Canada. I remember humorously asking a chaplain on one of the campuses about his job description. He replied, "Loitering with intent!" While I wasn't actually loitering I was spending a lot of time with students, listening, pondering, and engaging them with their life purposes. One student in particular seemed curious about the Christian way. He offered me a big challenge. He said to me, "Would you let me hang around you for a few days? Just be with you? I want to find out what it is like on the inside to be in the Christian family and to be in the kingdom of God before I commit." He wanted to experience the evidence.

The kingdom of God is the incursion into this life and into this world of the dynamic and shalom-bringing rule of God. It is the life of the world to come interpenetrating life in this world. It is the new world coming in both senses of that word: coming now and coming in the future. It is a

1. Quoted in Sherman, *Kingdom Calling*, 33–34.
2. Laing, *Politics of Experience and the Bird of Paradise*, 15.

joyous new reality with Jesus at the center. But it is not just composed of people, people whom the apostle John called "companions in the kingdom" (Rev 1:9). As well as people it is a place—yes even a physical and social reality. It is actually a place, a people, and a presence (the presence of God). So it involves the transformation of the world and people under the sway of Jesus as King.

It is God's gift of shalom, a beautiful biblical term that communicates more than simply peace of mind or cessation of conflict. It is human, social, and creational flourishing. Cornelius Plantinga Jr. defines *shalom*:

> The webbing together of God, humans, and all creation in justice, fulfillment, and delight is what the Hebrew prophets call *shalom*. We call it peace, but it means far more than mere peace of mind or a cease-fire between enemies. In the Bible, shalom means *universal flourishing, wholeness, and delight*—a rich state of affairs in which natural needs are satisfied and natural gifts fruitfully employed, a state of affairs that inspires joyful wonder as its Creator and Savior opens doors and welcomes the creatures in whom he delights. Shalom, in other words, is the way things ought to be.[3]

But like my student who wanted to stick around me to find out what it was really like, we want to know what the kingdom is like before we enter it. This is something Jesus understood and addressed. To speak of this new reality Jesus used metaphors, which are ways of drawing meaning from one reality and applying to another, so bringing greater depth.

Attending a Fun Party

I have never been a perennial partygoer but I can tell you I have enjoyed the ones I have attended. For example, there was the seventieth wedding anniversary party of my parents-in-law, which we held in the atrium of Regent College. The food was great, presented by a local social enterprise that provides employment for single moms. All the extended family and some long-standing friends were there, some traveling halfway across Canada to make the scene. There were some speeches and lots of good humor. The youngest grandchildren had fun taking the elevator up and down from the ground floor. We took pictures which we still treasure, especially one of the honored couple, Dad smiling with a flower in his lapel and Mom, impeccably dressed as always, with her glasses on (but she was losing her sight). We

3. Quoted in Alexander and Brown, eds., *To Whom Shall We Go?*, 35.

all went home exhilarated. The kingdom is like that. Or it is like our sixtieth wedding anniversary party, when all our children and grandchildren, many of them with spouses, celebrated over a fantastic meal with Gail and me. So, says Jesus, the kingdom is like a wedding banquet a king gives at the marriage of his son (Matt 22:2). People of all ages are there (Matt 8:11). Fun!

This is hinted at in an Old Testament passage describing what to do with one's tithe. If you live a long way from Jerusalem, so goes the text, and cannot bring animals and birds to the joyous festival in Jerusalem, "exchange your tithe for silver" and with the silver "buy whatever you like: cattle, sheep, wine and other fermented drink, or anything you wish. Then you and your household shall eat in the presence of the Lord your God and rejoice" (Deut 14:24–26). This is not a text pastors usually read before the offering is taken up in church!

But the kingdom party is composed of an odds-and-sods group of people, "the bad as well as the good" (Matt 22:10), as Jesus tells us in one parable. Some of these people have been compelled to come in from the back lanes and streets of the city—many of those invited did not want to come—but the party must be full.

From the beginning (like now) to the end (when everything gets wrapped up) Jesus said the kingdom is like a party. Jesus' first miracle was turning water into wine at a wedding in Cana of Galilee. In fact he made a lot of really good wine, eighty gallons of the best wine by some calculations. The final image of the kingdom come in the book of the Revelation is, once again, a wedding party, a picture of life in the new heaven and new earth. "Hallelujah! For our Lord God Almighty reigns. Let us rejoice and be glad and give him glory. For the wedding of the Lamb [a metaphor for Jesus] has come, and his bride [a metaphor for the church] has made herself ready" (Rev 19:6–7). In heaven—really the new heaven and new earth—we will experience a *continuous* party in which we eat and drink with Jesus (Matt 26:29). Jesus said to his first followers, and to us, "I confer on you a kingdom, just as my Father conferred one on me, so that you may eat and drink at my table in my kingdom" (Luke 22:29). Who would not want to come? But maybe there are some.

Finding a Precious Treasure

One Catholic theologian said, sadly, that the thought of going to heaven left him bored. I can appreciate this. If the kingdom of heaven, also called the kingdom of God, is being a soul floating in ether and singing the same worship song six million times over and again, I am not sure I want to go there. But such is a gross misunderstanding of the new heaven and the new earth and even the kingdom now. So, says Jesus, it is like this: a person was plowing a neighbor's field and the plowshare struck a box buried in the ground. The farmer stopped the animal and took a good look. Yes, it was a box. He dug around it, pulled it out, and opened the clasp. It was full of gold! Wow! So what did he do? He reburied the treasure, went and sold everything he had—a metaphor of the cost of discipleship to Jesus—liquidated his assets, and with the money bought the field in order to get the treasure (Matt 13:44). It is worth everything. But this is not the only image of discovery Jesus used.

Discovering the kingdom of God is like being a pearl merchant. This connoisseur of fine pearls goes from agent to agent, market to market, looking for the best ones to buy, and later to sell. I have been to a pearl market in Manila, looking for the best string to buy for my wife, Gail. (It is not surprising that so many of the parables of Jesus are placed in the marketplace, in the arena of human exchange. After all, he was a merchant himself, selling his ability to design and build houses, cradles, or tables. And the marketplace figures in much if not most of his teaching.) But this pearl merchant discovers something he has never before seen, a magnificent pearl in hue, density, shape, and color. And it was big, the biggest he had ever seen. He has been looking for this all his working life. And here it is right before his eyes. Can he have it? Only if he sells everything he has and buys it (Matt 13:45–6). Which he does. And is he satisfied with giving up everything to get the best? You bet he is.

So why is the kingdom a precious treasure for which a person will abandon her or his old way of life, and all their possessions, in order to gain, and for what? Here is what. The kingdom is the best thing ever. We become more human. People flourish. *Inside* we have peace, forgiveness, joy, and, would you believe, contentment. *Outside* we have purpose. We have an amazing vocation of loving God and neighbor in the particular and fulfilling way we were each made by the Creator. And the joy of that discovery never wears off. It gets better day by day. Who would not want it? But there is even more.

Experiencing an Explosion of Goodness

The kingdom, Jesus said, is something that brings potent change, good change, and constant change. It is like yeast folded into dough, exploding the dough but making the bread wonderfully digestible (Matt 13:33). You cannot see it happening but you see the effect; it becomes a beautiful loaf, not just a flatbread. My grandfather was a baker and I like this metaphor especially. And, further, Jesus said the kingdom is like putting a key into a lock and guess what, the door opens (Matt 16:19). It like throwing an ember from a fire into a forest with lots of undergrowth and, you guessed it, that tiny spark produced a forest fire (Luke 12:49). It is like putting salt on a roast that is "just on the turn" and almost inedible, but with salt you love it and devour it (Matt 5:13). It brings the taste out. The kingdom is like lighting an oil lamp in a completely darkened room—or turning on an LED in the garage—and with the light you can see everything (Matt 5:14–16). It is like going into a field with a sack full of tiny seeds around your waist and distributing them into the turned up soil, only to find weeks later, they have grown hugely. Indeed some of the new growth is large enough for birds to land in (Matt 13:1–9, 31–32).

So, not surprisingly, the apostle Paul says "the kingdom is not a matter of talk but of power"(1 Cor 4:20). Yet in spite of this powerful transformation the kingdom is not fully visible now (Luke 17:20). It is, as Paul says, a "heavenly" kingdom (2 Tim 4:18). "My kingdom is not of this world," says Jesus (John 18:36). So in this age the kingdom is mixed in with anti-kingdom realities (weeds in a wheat field), to be separated and judged on the last day (Matt 13:24–30, 40–43, 47–50), or like a like a farmer separating sheep and goats (Matt 25:31–46).

But in spite of being largely invisible except for the church, the kingdom demands a response right now and clashes with the status quo. To elaborate on the challenge Jesus told the story of a king who wanted to settle accounts with his servants, showing mercy to a debtor who got forgiven a massive amount but ultimately rejecting the forgiven person who was unmerciful to someone who owed him a fraction of what he had been forgiven (Matt 18:23–35). Jesus said the kingdom was like a landowner who pays everyone the same wages, even though some have worked longer, showing incredible generosity (Matt 20:1–16). The kingdom is like a person who invests bags of gold in servants to see what they will do with it (Matt 25:14–30), the five-talent person making it exceedingly fruitful, a further fivefold in fact. So the kingdom is a disruptive force.

The kingdom disrupts the present religious, social, political, economic, and physical orders, turning the world upside down, really right side up. It brings God's shalom, a holistic peace and restoration of health and flourishing—but in doing so brings disruption. Yet the disruption is partial because, while the kingdom *has come, it has not yet come fully, and will not come fully until Christ returns and the end has come.* It is now and not yet, here but coming. So at the moment it is hidden like a tiny seed, and mixed into the realities of the world, but it will grow explosively. South American theologian Mortimer Arias puts it this way:

> The coming of the kingdom means a permanent confrontation of worlds. The kingdom is a question mark in the midst of established ideas and answers developed by peoples and societies. The kingdom is an irreverent exposure of human motivations and of the most sacred rules of human mores. The kingdom is an iconoclastic disturber of religious sacred places and customs and the most radical threat to temple altars, priestly castes, and the most protected "holy of holies." The kingdom is the appointed challenger of all sacralizing myths and systems and the relentless unmasker of all human disguises, self-righteous ideologies, or self-perpetuating powers.[4]

So this potent transformation comes with a price tag: trouble. Is it worth it to have this potent transformation—as it was for Jesus "who for the joy set before him he endured the cross" (Heb 12:2)? And the kingdom is about the King.

Experiencing a Transformative Person

Jesus embodied the kingdom. Some early church fathers used the Greek word *autobasileia* to describe Jesus—the kingdom of God in his own person. If we simply look at Jesus we discover that the kingdom is spiritual but more than spiritual. It is holistic, bringing transformation to every part of life and ultimately to creation itself. The renewal of everything is the vision of Ephesians 1. In one of the Paul's long sentences he starts his letter to the Ephesians by saying: "Praise be to the God and Father of our Lord Jesus Christ . . . to bring unity to all things in heaven and on earth under Christ" (1:3, 10). The final word of Jesus in the last book of the Bible is the greatest renewal text in all Scripture: "I am making everything new" (Rev 21:5). But

4. Arias, *Announcing the Reign of God*, 46–47.

in the down-to-earth ministry of Jesus we see the holism of the kingdom as indicated by the words and deeds of Jesus.

It is spiritual—"Your sins are forgiven," said Jesus (Mark 2:9). It is personal—"I will give you rest for your souls," (Matt 11:28). It is social. In answer to John's disciples, Jesus said, "The blind recover their sight, the lame walk, those who have leprosy are cleansed, the deaf hear, the dead are raised, and the good news is proclaimed to the poor" (Matt 11:5). It has political-cosmic dimensions. Speaking of the Pharisees, Jesus said, "They tie up heavy, cumbersome loads and put them on other people's shoulders" (Matt 23:4); and Jesus overturned the table of money changers in the temple (Matt 21:12). It is economic, for when Zaccheus the tax collector welcomed Jesus into his home he blurted out, "If I have cheated anybody . . . I will pay back four times the amount" (Luke 19:8). Soul salvation? Yes, of course, but even better the kingdom of God is the whole good news.

So that is what the kingdom is like. Is it worth it to get into it, to serve it, to embrace its life and calling, and even to embrace the cross? That is a fair question, one which Jesus himself was asked by the disciple Peter: What do we get out of it? "We have left everything to follow you! What then will there be for us?" asked Peter. To this Jesus gives an answer that has two levels, partially for now and ultimately in what he calls "the renewal of all things" (Matt 19:28).[5]

> Truly I tell you, no one who has left home or brothers or sisters or mother or father or children or fields for me and the gospel will fail to receive a hundred times as much in this present age: home, brothers, sisters, mothers, children and fields—along with persecutions—and in the age to come eternal life. But many who are first will be last, and the last first (Mark 10:29–31).

So is it worth it? Why not try hanging around believers to find out. Or better still, go directly to Jesus and ask him to show himself to you, and to reveal his kingdom. It is too good to miss.

---

5. Compare Matthew 19:27–30 and its future orientation with Mark 10:29–31 and its present orientation.

PART TWO

Bringing in the Kingdom in the Marketplace

4

How the Kingdom Comes —God's Initiative

A Survey from Genesis to Revelation

"We cannot simply take the Kingdom by the arm and 'usher it in'; only God can do that."

—JOHN BRIGHT[1]

THOUGH THE TERM "KINGDOM of God" is not always used in Scripture, from the beginning God intended to exercise his sovereignty through his entire creation and his creature. He purposed humankind to flourish, commissioning his God-imaging creature (humankind) to flesh out the good interest of God in all of life and the entirety of creation. "The vision of Yahweh's kingdom permeated all of life in ancient Israel" (Exod 19:5–6; Ps 103:19; Mic 4:2–3), says Charles Ringma, a colleague of mine.[2] It seems that God at creation had a final end in view. God apparently had in mind from the very beginning of creation the wedding supper of the Lamb, that glorious and joyful rendezvous of God, the people of God, and the land (Rev 19:7). So Jesus spoke about "the kingdom prepared for you since the creation of the world" (Matt 25:34). To accomplish that God made humankind, male and female, commissioned them, and when they sinned, sent

1. Bright, *Kingdom of God*, 169.
2. Ringma, oral lecture, 2008.

his own Son to remedy the situation. He will come again to fully establish the kingdom. The kingdom is not an afterthought.

This and the next chapter are theological in character, but as the Puritan William Perkins once said, "theology of the science of living blessedly forever."[3] And Charlie Brown once commented that there is nothing quite so comforting as good theology.

In this summary of God's initiative in bringing in his kingdom I am drawing on, along with the Bible, the classic book that I first studied five decades ago: John Bright, *The Kingdom of God*. In this book he says, "The concept of the Kingdom of God involves, in a real sense, the total message of the Bible. . . . To grasp what is meant by the Kingdom of God is to come very close to the heart of the Bible's gospel of salvation."[4] But there was a problem.

Grace and the Recovery of the Kingdom Vocation

Sin disrupted the program. Work became toil. Humankind experimented with autonomy and died spiritually. Relationships got spoiled, even politicized. The first death was a murder. But God brings redemption. Old Testament professor Bruce Waltke, speaking of Genesis 3:15, says, "God's promise to establish his kingdom through his grace that overcomes human sin is the governing theme of Genesis. God promises a seed that will destroy the Serpent, entailing that through it [the seed of woman] humanity will gain the Paradise it lost."[5]

The descendants of Adam and Eve's sinful son, Cain, in a sense created the beginnings of civilization. Cain built a city and his descendents became the makers of commerce ("raise livestock"), crafts ("forged all kind of tools out of bronze and iron"), and culture ("play stringed instruments and pipes") (Gen 4:17–22). God had not abandoned his creation or his creature since he had made an irrevocable covenant—an agreement of mutual belonging—with his creation and his creature that involved three dimensions: communion with God, community-building ,and co-creativity.[6]

3. Perkins, *Golden Chain*, 177.

4. Bright, *Kingdom of God*, 7.

5. Waltke, *Genesis*, 50.

6. See Stevens, "Covenant Mandate." Communion with God is implied in the sanctuary and stated in Genesis 3:8: "Then the man and his wife heard the sound of the Lord God as he was walking in the garden in the cool of the day." It is a full-time job.

The Kingdom Covenant

Indeed when God found a righteous family in Noah and made a covenant with him, Old Testament scholar William Dumbrell notes that the phrase "I now establish my covenant with you and with your descendents after you" (Gen 9:8) has the sense of *renewing* the covenant already in existence.[7] Dumbrell concludes that there is only one divine covenant, which starts with Genesis 1:1 and ends with the renewal of all things in Revelation 21:5. "The world and man are part of one total divine construct and we cannot entertain the salvation of man in isolation from the world which he has affected."[8] This covenant is essentially unconditional—that is, God will not divorce his people or his creation. That said, the *blessings* of the covenant— especially the land and human flourishing—are conditional on obedience, which turns out to be God's issue with the human race. But God has not given up on either people or the creational project.

So God calls a family, the family of promise—Abraham, Isaac, and Jacob. The New Testament says that Abraham "was looking forward to the city with foundations, whose architect and builder is God" (Heb 11:10), anticipating the new Jerusalem "coming down out of heaven from God" (Rev 21:2). The promise and covenant given to Abraham had three parts: an immense family, the land, and the blessing of the Gentiles (Gen 12:2–3;

Community-building is implied in the creation of woman as an equal and adequate to the man, and in the statement that "in the image of God he created them, male and female he created them" (1:27). This also is a full-time job, building community in family and society. Co-creativity is implied in the command to "rule over the fish of the sea . . . and over all creatures that move along the ground" (1:26) and "Be fruitful and increase in numbers; fill the earth and subdue it" (1:28). God the worker makes in God's image a human being who will work and unpack the potential of creation and "take care of it" (2:15), another full-time job. For a more complete outline of the covenant mandate see Stevens, *Other Six Days*, 91–105.

7. Dumbrell, "End of the Beginning." G. K. Beale comments: "Dumbrell makes his most helpful and creative contributions in the area of covenant theology. Especially in this respect the author's present work is a further development of his earlier *Covenant and Creation* (Lancer/Paternoster, 1984), where he argues that the diverse expressions of covenant(s) throughout the Bible are but aspects of 'only one biblical covenant, that made implicitly by the fact of creation itself and reestablished in the details of Gen. 6:18 and 9:7–13' (*cf. End of the Beginning*, p. 103). Dumbrell makes a good case that all the covenants and promises after the Abrahamic are primarily intended as positive developments of that covenant (*e.g.* pp. 49–52, 97–99, 129, 134, 149, 195). Likewise, the Abrahamic covenant is placed after the preceding chapters of Genesis as a keynote explaining how the problems introduced by the fall will be resolved (*cf.* p. 132)."

8. Dumbrell, *Covenant and Creation*, 41.

15:7; 17:8)—the proof positive that while the kingdom of God was to be mainly a family composed of all the nations of the earth, it was also the renewal and development of the land. And all the promises of God find their "Yes" in Christ (2 Cor 1:20). But, when famine comes, the family of promise descended into Egypt hunting for food.

In Egypt, first under the rule of Joseph, Jacob's son, and then, when Joseph was no longer known, the now numerous Hebrew family in Egypt became slaves. But they also became a nation through Moses, the rescued offspring of a Hebrew mother. Psalm 114:1–2 says, "When Israel came out of Egypt, Jacob from a people of foreign tongue, Judah became God's sanctuary, Israel his dominion," thus with sanctuary and dominion combining all three of the dimensions of the covenant code: communion, community-building, and co-creativity. Through the exodus, and the mighty deliverance of the people of God at the Red Sea, and the years of "wandering in the wilderness"—a trip that should have taken two years but because the people were unready to possess the land, took a generation—they are poised to enter the land of Canaan and take possession. This is where Rahab comes into the story, this double agent for the kingdom of God who protected the two spies Joshua sent in. The account of the invasion and possession is stretched out and nuanced with some of the original inhabitants who remained influencing the people of God but not for their good. Bright puts it this way: "The occupation of Palestine was thus partly a process of absorption which went on at least until David consolidated the entire land."[9]

Having a king "like all the other nations" was both a success—it produced David, a person after God's own heart—and a failure, in that most of the monarchs did not represent God's interests on earth. During this time an official state-supported religion—in which the religion begins to hallow the state in the name of God—had been created, something which the prophets at great personal risk resisted. "With Amos," Bright says, "the rejection of that blasphemous identification of the people and the kingdom of God with the Israelite state has become total. . . . *The Kingdom of Israel is not the Kingdom of God.*"[10] Jeremiah laments: "A horrible and shocking thing has happened in the land: The prophets prophesy lies, the priests rule by their own authority, and my people love it this way. But what will you do in the end?" (Jer 5:30–31). But Hosea, brooding with the heart of God over

9. Bright, *Kingdom of God*, 23.

10. Bright, *Kingdom of God*, 66–67, emphasis his.

a sick society and a sick church, proposes that while "the people's *hesed* may fail, God's will never!"[11]

The Remnant as the Kingdom

New superpowers threatened the nation now under judgment. Assyria took the northern kingdom into captivity, literally displacing the intelligentsia, the rich, and the leaders to a foreign land and leaving the poor to till the ground for the new owners. And later, the southern kingdom tumbled to the latest superpower, Babylon, who again took the best people into captivity. Here I draw on John Bright: "The notion of a pure Remnant of God's people, cleansed in the fiery trial and made amendable to God's purpose, is one of the most characteristic ideas of Isaiah (4:2–4; 10:20–22; 37:30–32), and one that was to exert a profound influence on his people for centuries to come."[12] Bright concludes his chapter on "A Remnant Shall Repent" with these apt words:

> As civilization and material property, nations and churches, are tossed into the caldron there is always a Remnant, a people of God, a true church. And with these God works his will. To them he says, "Fear not, little flock, for it is your father's good pleasure to give you the kingdom" (Luke 12:32).[13]

Jeremiah, who had not lost hope in that coming kingdom, foretold of a new covenant that would be made with Israel and Judah with the law written on people's hearts (Jer 31:31–37). Some of the prophets, notably Daniel who was in exile with their failed nation, envisioned the passing of all human kingdoms and the coming of the kingdom of God that would never end, bringing eternal shalom and well-being.

The Kingdom Is Holistic

We are seeing that the kingdom of God is the dominant theme of the entire Bible. Psalm 93:1–4, for example, says "The Lord Reigns, he is robed in majesty. . . . the seas have lifted up their voice. . . . Mightier than the thunder of the great waters . . . the Lord on high is mighty." Over and over again

11. Bright, *Kingdom of God*, 76.
12. Bright, *Kingdom of God*, 89.
13. Bright, *Kingdom of God*, 97.

the psalmist proclaims, "Our God reigns." Indeed, contrary to the usual understanding of "Be still, and know that I am God" (46:10), this exhortation is not spoken to the believer to seek silence and solitude—a good thing to do—but to the powers raging in their opposition to the rule of God—political, social, cosmic, spiritual powers that form an anti-kingdom. But this universal emphasis on the rule of God is not just expressed in the Psalms. Isaiah 52:7 notes, "How beautiful in the mountains are the feet of those who bring good news. . . . 'Your God reigns.'" It would, nevertheless, be unthinkable to the Old Testament saint to say that the kingdom of God would be solely and only "spiritual" or "soulish." The kingdom was for the Old Testament believer the rule of the sovereign in all of life and in the total creation. But with the New Testament we enter a new phase of kingdom coming.

At the end of the Old Testament there is a people living paradoxically with apocalypse—that the kingdom of God is definitely not humankind's doing. Then, secondly, there was Phariseeism and the law—that the kingdom will come as people live obediently to the law and live righteously. Ironically a third option was that the kingdom could come by violent revolution, through which the hated Roman governor would be ousted, an option Jesus flatly rejected (John 6:15). Into this situation comes Jesus, who seamlessly wove together two strands of prophecy in the Old Testament which, so far as we know, had never before been connected: the Messiah King (the Anointed One, Ps 2:7; 110:1) and the Suffering Servant (Isa 42:1; 52:13–53:12). Fragments of these two strands were combined in the word from the Father to Jesus at his baptism and on the Mount of Transfiguration. "This is my son, whom I love; with him I am well pleased"(Matt 3:17; see also 17:5).[14] But Jesus was to start his messianic calling by following a strange figure from the desert whose one vocation was to prepare the way for the Lord.

Changing the Tense of the Kingdom Announcement

The radical message of John the Baptist was addressed to people who thought they were already in God's kingdom by being simply circumcised and attending the temple. John disenfranchised the entire nation and said

---

14. "At Christ's baptism and transfiguration the Father proclaimed Him both Son and Servant in words drawn from this verse [Psalm 2:7] and from Isaiah 42:1 (Matt 3:17; 17:5; 2 Pet 1:17)." Kidner, *Psalms 1–72*, 51.

that people were not in the kingdom unless they repented, were baptized, and waited for the coming Messiah. And Jesus was that Messiah. So the verbal tense changes from the Old Testament—"the kingdom *is* coming"—to the New Testament—"the kingdom *has* come" (Mark 1:14–15). But, Bright continues, "The two Testaments are organically linked to each other.... And the bond that binds them together is the rule of God."[15] There is, nevertheless, this new fact that now the kingdom of God is embodied in Jesus, who in his home synagogue after the reading of Isaiah 61 said, "Today this is fulfilled in your hearing" (Luke 4:16–21). But Jesus is not the kind of Messiah-King the people of Israel expected. He combined the Suffering Servant of Isaiah 42–53 with the Son of Man or the heavenly man, in Daniel 7:13–14, and claimed to be the Son of God (Luke 4:3), ruling through service, crucifixion, resurrection, and ascension. New Testament scholar I. Howard Marshall says, "Not surprisingly motifs from several Old Testament passages . . . provided the pattern for the destiny of Jesus [and] are coalesced to give a picture of him as the suffering, vindicated and authoritative Son of Man."[16] But why did Jesus so designate himself?[17]

The Son of Man and the Kingdom Mission of God

N. T. Wright says that Jesus used the title Son of Man in a way that was a "constant, albeit veiled, self-reference."[18] To describe himself Jesus used the Son of Man figure of Daniel 7 as his favorite self-designation—"The Son of Man did not come to be served, but to serve, and to give his life as a ransom for many" (Mark 10:45). This could have been heard as meaning simply "I" but, as Wright says, "There is good evidence that this figure, Israel's representative, was already by the time of Jesus regarded by some as messianic . . . although Jesus was engaged in filling this title, too, with fresh meaning."[19] So, in Daniel's vision of 7 the Son of Man "coming with the clouds of heaven" approaches the Ancient of Days (God the Father) and is given "authority, glory and sovereign power; *all nations and peoples of every language worshipped him. His dominion is an everlasting dominion*

15. Bright, *Kingdom of God*, 196–7.

16. Marshall, "Son of Man," 776.

17. For example, in the Gospel of Mark the phrase occurs fourteen times: Mark 2:10, 28; 8:31, 38; 9:9, 12, 31; 10:33, 45; 13:26; 14:21 a, b, 41, 62.

18. Wright, "Jesus," 349.

19. Wright, "Jesus," 350.

that will not pass away . . ." (Dan 7:13–14, emphasis mine). This vision of all-encompassing worship is the vision the early Christian disciple Stephen had.

Significantly, Stephen, who is known as the first Christian martyr, is also the first missionary, since, as they stoned him to death, he envisioned the resurrected Jesus as "the Son of Man standing at the right hand of God" (Acts 7:56), meaning that Jesus is reaching out to everyone. His kingdom is not restricted to the Jewish people or to the temple. This made Stephen's accusers so enraged at this perceived blasphemy—a human being, Jesus, Stephen was claiming to be God—that they killed him. In the Acts record of the event all three persons of the Trinity are present: God the Father (the Ancient of Days), Jesus the Son (the Son of Man), and the Holy Spirit that filled Stephen (Acts 7:55), since the Holy Spirit makes Jesus known and communicates the truth of the Gospel. Stephen attested to the outgoingness, the mission of God. The triune God is both in-going and out-going.

The Trinity and the Kingdom

On the first, the in-going of God, God is a "lover, the beloved and the love itself," as Jürgen Moltmann put it, reflecting on a phrase from Augustine.[20] On the second, the out-going of God, in Scripture God is sender, sent, and sending.[21] So Jesus commissions his followers with these revealing words: "As the Father has *sent* me, I am *sending* you" (John 20:21). There is, in the fourth Gospel, over forty instances of sending *within* God and *by* God. The English word *mission* comes from the Latin *missio*, which simply means "to send." This rich understanding of the Godhead as sender, sent, and sending contributes to our understanding of God as on mission in the establishment of his kingdom. Each of three persons of the Godhead contributes to the forming of the kingdom of God. The Father creates, providentially sustains, and forms a covenantal framework for all existence. The Son incarnates, mediates, transfigures, and redeems. The Spirit empowers and fills with God's own presence. But each shares in the others—coinheres, interpenetrates, cooperates—so that it is theologically and practically inappropriate to stereotype the ministry or mission to one of the three exclusively. As Colin Gunton notes, there is "reciprocity, interpenetration and

20. Moltmann, *Trinity and the Kingdom*, 32.
21. Stevens, *Abolition of the Laity*, 57.

interanimation"[22] in all three persons. So, if the essence of God is relationship—a communion of being and doing—God is more one *because* God is three. God is family (Eph 3:15) with each person pouring into the life of the other. The fourth-century Cappadocian fathers (Basil, Gregory of Nyssa, and Gregory of Nazianzus) spoke of this mystery by using the Greek term *perichoresis*, a term that suggests a dance with-in and with-out God, a reciprocity, interchange, and receiving without blurring of identities. So whose kingdom is it—the Father's, the Son's, or the Spirit's?

The kingdom of God is the kingdom of God, Father, Son, and Holy Spirit. When the psalmist declares: "Let the people of Zion be glad in their King (Ps 149:2) it is the triune God who is ruler. So the phrase Son of Man was enigmatically chosen as a title by Jesus most frequently to cull out misunderstandings about the kingdom and the King, which people had viewed as a political entity, particularly ridding Israel of Rome. Jesus announced that in his coming, death, resurrection, ascension, and the outpouring of the Spirit, the kingdom has begun to come *in a new way*. Stephen grasped that, as did John in the Revelation—the more-than-Jewishness of the kingdom.[23] For that reason I spoke of Stephen as the first missionary.[24] But it is the Spirit who confirms that people belong to God and his kingdom whenever they cry Abba in prayer (Rom 8:15–16); the Spirit who leads us in vocational discernment, in planning and execution as the Apostle Paul knew when he decided not to go to certain locations even when there was a door of opportunity (Acts 16:6–8); and the Spirit that anoints creational talents for more effective and excellent work (Rom 12:6–9). It is the Spirit who inspires creativity in the workplace, as was the case with Bezalel (Exod 31:2–5); and the Spirit who enables us to overcome the internal and external struggles we experience in life in this world and turns these into

22. Gunton, *One, the Three and the Many*, 163 (emphasis mine).

23. Other references to the Son of Man in the New Testament include Acts 7:56; Heb 2:6; Rev 1:13; 14:14. In 1 Enoch and 4 Ezra the Son of Man is positively identified with the Messiah, God's Son and elect one. "It was . . . a term which would not have been meaningful for non-Jews. Since modern readers on the whole do not pick up the original nuances of the term (whether as a self-designation or as an allusion to Dan 7), the example of the early church in not using it remains valid today. There is indeed a grave danger of using 'Son of man' as a means of referring to the humanity of Jesus as opposed to his divinity (expressed by 'Son of God'), whereas in fact the Danielic background suggests a figure closely associated with the Ancient of Days." Marshall, "Son of Man," 781.

24. In fact the old man Simeon at the blessing of baby Jesus was the first "missionary" to see the more-than-Jewishness of the kingdom when he affirmed that this Jesus would be a "light for revelation to the Gentiles" (Luke 2:32).

spiritual growth (Gal 5:19–25). The Spirit brings hope for the full coming of the kingdom (Rev 1:10); and the Spirit brings joy (Matt 25:23). But having said that, Father, Son, and Holy Spirit are united in kingdom inauguration, God establishing the kingdom especially through the Messiah.

Jesus as Embodying the Kingdom of God

Bright insists that "the Messiah himself was never thought of apart from the Kingdom; when the Messiah comes the Kingdom comes."[25] So, summarizing the original good news of Jesus proclaimed by the first Christians, Bright proposes:

> It was a very simple gospel and very clear. It announced that the New Age of God proclaimed by the prophets had begun; that the long awaited Messiah had come, who is none other than this Jesus who did mighty works, died and rose again according to the Scriptures; that this Jesus has now been exalted to the highest heaven to sit at the right hand of God, from whence he shall shortly come again "to judge the quick and the dead."[26]

Jesus countered the religious-cultural view of the kingdom in a double way. He did not proclaim that the kingdom would violently wrest away the rule of the Roman government and, strangely, he did not affirm that people could bring in the kingdom through religious activity and moral righteousness, as the Pharisees taught. But he did not simply spiritualize the kingdom. One could argue that the "greater commission" is Luke 4:18–19 and the "greatest commission" is in John 20:21, a fully incarnational mission—thus fulfilling the creation mandate in Genesis. This includes not just the stewardship of creation but "filling the earth" (Gen 1:28), not only peopling the earth through procreation but co-creation, extending the sanctuary garden into the world, thereby bringing God's glory everywhere as the world is stewarded.

So Jesus briefed the early apostles (sent-out ones) on the kingdom of God before his ascension (Acts 1:3). Philip "proclaimed the good news of the kingdom of God" (Acts 8:12). Paul and Barnabas preached, "We must go through many hardships to enter the kingdom of God" (Acts 14:22).[27]

25. Bright, *Kingdom of God*, 216.

26. Bright, *Kingdom of God*, 190.

27. A few of the New Testament texts outside the Gospels, and especially of Paul and Peter, proclaiming the kingdom, are Acts 19:8; 20:25; 28:23, 31; Rom 14:17; 1 Cor 4:20;

Paul clearly stated that the whole people of God were called to the kingdom and its ministry: "God . . . calls you into his kingdom and glory" (1 Thess 2:12). The final vision in the New Testament, the Revelation, clearly is the kingdom having fully come: "The kingdom of the world has become the kingdom of our Lord and of his Messiah, and he will reign for ever and ever" (Rev 11:15). It is the dominant theme of the Bible. It sums up what God is about with his creation and his people, how he intends to rule everything and everyone with his gracious and good kingship. But it is more than spiritual. That is critical when it comes to the kingdom ministry of Jesus.

Jesus did not merely preach the gospel of soul salvation but rather proclaimed the *god-spel,* the "good tale" of the kingdom of God. He announced that the rule had already come, embodied in his own ministry and that of his disciples. So he said, "If I drive out demons by the finger of God, then the kingdom of God has come upon you" (Luke 11:20).[28] But the kingdom would come fully at the end. So in the indirect teaching of the parables of the kingdom and in direct teaching of the Lord, Jesus said repeatedly that the kingdom is a mystery revealed, long hidden from the eyes of humankind but now made plain.[29] The kingdom is here and now, and yet not (fully) here but coming. It is like a thin edge of a wedge driven into this age with the full wedge transforming everything when Jesus comes again at the end of history.

The Kingdom Fully Come

Revelation, the last book of the New Testament, provisions faith through the imagination, and points to the end in which Christ is King of kings and all reality—visible and invisible—has been subdued to God's gracious shalom-bringing rule. In that book the people of God, the earth, and all reality are transformed into a new (renewed) heaven and new (renewed

---

15:24; Gal 5:21; Col 1:13; Heb 12:28; Jas 2:5; 2 Pet 1:11.

28. France, *Divine Government,* 29.

29. George Eldon Ladd, as we have noted previously, explains the mystery of the kingdom this way: "The kingdom of God is here but not with irresistible power. The kingdom has come, but it is not like a stone grinding an image to powder. On the contrary, it is like a man sowing seed. It does not force itself upon men." Ladd, *Gospel of the Kingdom,* 56.

earth). Dumbrell's reviewer G. K. Beale notes appreciatively how, in *The End of the Beginning*, each of the themes the author explores are an

> aspect of the Bible's wider concept of government, the Kingdom of God. . . . The New Jerusalem is the symbol of government and those governed; the New Temple is the seat of government; the New Covenant is the instrument of government; the New Israel reveals those governed and their role; and the New Creation is a final comprehensive presentation of both the governed and the Governor.[30]

Thus the kingdom of God is the unifying theme of the entire Bible. So all who are engaged by Christ in this kingdom will be on a kingdom mission until that day when the King comes again—to which we say, along with early Christians, "Maranatha," Lord come.

Now, having explored God's determination to intervene and bring in his kingdom on earth, we must consider what the human vocation is in relation to it. Do we have a part to play in the advancement of God's rule on earth and in people's lives, especially in the marketplace?

30. Cited in Dumbrell, *End of the Beginning*, Introduction.

5

How the Kingdom Comes
—Humankind's Initiative

"Unless the Lord builds the house, the builders labor in vain."

—Solomon, Psalm 127:1

"God without us will not, as we without God cannot."

—Augustine[1]

I WAS SITTING ON the sidewalk outside an ice cream parlor in my city, chatting with the owner. Vanilla ice cream is my one weakness! No other flavor is worth trying. While we sat there in the sun talking, the owner spoke with about half of the passersby on the sidewalk, obviously knowing many of them by name, as well as their life situations. I was impressed but said nothing. Then he turned to me and said, "You know, Paul, I am not sure what my life purpose is."

I responded, "David (not his real name), long ago Jesus said that the purpose of our lives is to 'love God with all our heart, with all our strength and mind, and to love our neighbor as ourselves.' Of course we each do this in a very special way. But, David, you *are* loving your neighbors; you have a fine ice cream product, you personally care for your customers, and you care for the people in your community."

1. Quoted in Sherman, *Kingdom Calling,* 238.

I could have continued to suggest that he was doing it in a kingdom way, even though he was a not-yet Christian. But, and here I am asking a serious question, could I have said: "You are doing kingdom work." What is the relationship of what he was and is doing to the kingdom of God?

There is a stunning passage in a South American theologian Mortimer Arias, which I will try to apply to the present context in brackets:

> Jesus meant that the kingdom cannot be ensured by faithfully observing rites and ceremonies in the Temple of Jerusalem, as the priests and Sadducees claimed [or as is common today, by becoming a religious functionary]; it cannot be earned by strictly observing the law and its rabbinic interpretations, as the Pharisees taught [or by obtaining a deep personal spirituality with disciplines and religious practices]; it cannot be secured by fleeing from the world to a secluded life of 'purity' in the wilderness, as the Essenes attempted [or by withdrawing from the world into a monastery or by spending your life in a Christian bubble]; it cannot be conquered by the piercing swords of the violent rebellion against Rome, as the Zealots pretended [or by engaging in social revolution and civil disobedience to secure rights]. The kingdom of God comes as grace, and it has to be received as a gift.[2]

But this leaves us with a crucial question. How does the kingdom actually come? Is it all God's work, God's gift, as Arias says? Or can we bring the kingdom to our neighbor? Or is there a symphony of wills and initiatives?

From the previous chapter it seems the kingdom comes by God's direct action. We receive and enter.[3] But can we also *bring in* the kingdom, or work with God in so doing? Revisiting the kingdom story from Genesis to Revelation, we find that humankind is given *some agency in bringing in the kingdom but in communion with God.*

---

2. Arias, *Announcing the Reign of God*, 17.

3. George Eldon Ladd in his classic work on the subject says, "The Kingdom of God is a miracle. It is the act of God.... Men cannot build the Kingdom.... It is God's reign.... The fruitage is produced not by human effort or skill but by the life of the Kingdom itself. It is God's deed." But he concludes later, drawing on Luke 10:9, 17, "Thus the Kingdom of God was at work among men not only in the person of our Lord but also through His disciples as they brought the word and the signs of the Kingdom to the cities of Galilee." Ladd, *Gospel of the Kingdom*, 64, 115.

Kings and Queens in the Garden

The Bible starts with God the worker fashioning all creation and, in particular, a garden sanctuary. Then God makes a creature "like himself," "in his
image," and places that image in the temple-garden, just as, in the ancient
world, the image of the god—be it Diana or whomever—would be placed
in the center of the sanctuary. The difference is that this "image" has feet,
heart, soul, and hands that can work. So under the Old Testament, God
in Genesis created human beings to rule, to take care of the world, and
to fill the earth with his glory. In effect those seminal passages in Genesis
1:28 and 2:15—"fill the earth and subdue it . . . rule . . . work it and take
care of it"—are God saying, "Work with me and in harmony with my purposes in bringing in the kingdom, developing the potential of creation and
bringing human flourishing everywhere. In doing so you will fill the world
with my glory." In calling humankind to "rule"(Gen 1:28) over everything
except themselves God made Adam and Eve and their descendants vice-
regents over everything on earth. Regents serve the monarch when the king
or queen is out of the country or too young to serve. Bruce Waltke in his
grand *Old Testament Theology* expresses it this way: "Genesis 1 confers this
authoritative status of God's image to all human beings, so that we are all
kings, given the responsibility to rule as God's vice-regents and high priests
on earth."[4] That is, the man and woman were to *bring in* God's kingdom, to
exhibit his rule "with power to control and regulate it, to harness its clear
potential, a tremendous concentration of power in the hands of puny man!
What authority he thus possesses to regulate the course of nature, to be a
bane or a blessing to the world!," says William Dumbrell, former dean at
Regent College.[5]

The garden as a sanctuary was a place of beauty, flourishing, and safety.
According to the text, the garden was *in* Eden (not as in Ezekiel where it is
said the garden is *of* Eden). So Eden appears in Genesis to be a larger reality
than the sanctuary garden; Eden is the *home* of Adam and Eve. And Eden
exists, in the Genesis account, in the larger reality of "other lands" such as
Havilah, "where there is gold" (Gen 2:11–12), in other words the *world* at
large. So without actually using the following words, the first human beings
were called, while "filling" the earth, to extend the presence, the rule, and
the glory of God into the entire world—bringing the sanctuary into the

4. Waltke, *Old Testament Theology*, 218.
5. Dumbrell, "Creation, Covenant and Work," 17.

world. Talk about a missionary calling! But the calling got messed up, not just in Genesis 3 in the so-called fall of humankind, but in the monarchy in the promised land.

The Kingdom in a Failed Nation

As a nation the Israelites were to embody God's rule in a spiritual-social-political-creational reality that involved a winsome lifestyle that would make them a light to the nations around. Indeed the total character of the kingdom is apparent in the so-called "covenant code" of Deuteronomy 12 to 30, which includes everything from serving one God (Deut 13), accurate weights and measures (read "reliable currency," 25:15), and servant leadership (17:14–20). This last mention—the king who would not think of himself as better than others—is significant as God's original intention was that God would directly rule his people. This is apparent in the response of the charismatic leader and savior-judge, Gideon, whom the people wanted to make into a king. But Gideon answered, "I will not rule over you, nor will my son rule over you. The Lord will rule over you" (Judg 8:23). Later the people demanded a king "like all the nations" and they got Saul as king (1 Sam 8:5). This project both succeeded and failed, as the people eventually were overcome by surrounding nations. John Bright puts it tersely: "In the process charisma gave way to dynasty."[6] But God wove his purpose into this human action and ultimately came in the Messiah as the son of David.

The failure was, nevertheless, spectacular. The covenant demanded *hesed*, the untranslatable Hebrew word that comes out awkwardly in English as "loving-kindness" but really unites love and faithfulness in a covenant relationship. *Hesed* is the glue of the covenant: affectionate loyalty. And *hesed* was conspicuously lacking in a people that worshipped other gods and idols, who perverted their lifestyle and in no way were a light to the Gentiles. The prophets spoke to this at great personal risk: Amos, Hosea, Isaiah, and Jeremiah. The prophets had the heart of God but that heart of judgment was also a heart of mercy and indicated that God had not abandoned his people, even though the nation would fail. So at the death of King Solomon, famed for wisdom but also famed for extracting everything he could from the people to finance his extravagant building projects, the kingdom of Israel divides into two, the northern kingdom keeping the name Israel and the southern kingdom taking its name from the main tribe,

6. Bright, *Kingdom of God*, 39.

Judah. Civil war took place. Then the northern kingdom was taken into exile, and later the southern kingdom.

The exile was not the end of Israel's faith. Indeed, during the exile an absolutely unique vision for the kingdom was supplied by Isaiah in the songs of the Suffering Servant (Isa 42–53). "The victory of that Kingdom, sure as God is sure, will be procured not by force or spectacular power, but by the sacrificial labor of God's Servant," said Bright.[7] Jesus saw himself as that Servant (Matt 12:15–21) and called his followers to serve one another as they served God. So Bright asks of our contemporary situation, "Can it be that we are seeking to build the Kingdom of the Servant—without following the Servant?"[8] The exile and even the restoration of Jerusalem under the Persian king Cyrus was, however, bitterly disappointing. Psalm 74 complains, "We are given no signs from God; no prophets are left, and none of us knows how long this will be" (v. 9).

Unpopular as the Servant vision of the kingdom was, there were two other strands of the kingdom developed during and because of the exile. The first was apocalyptic, that strange form of literature that thrived between 200 BC and 100 AD and of which the Revelation is our main biblical example, with dragons and beasts and great cosmic events portending the end, and of which Daniel is the premier Old Testament example. As we shall see, apocalypse ("revelation," or "exposé") is how the world looks to a person in the Spirit. Through apocalypse the vision of the kingdom of God is reshaped and shown to be triumphant—but triumphant strictly at God's hand. That is, as Bright says, "We cannot simply take the Kingdom by the arm and 'usher it in'; only God can do that."[9]

But the second kingdom development during the exile and restoration (after which some returned to Jerusalem and rebuilt the community, the wall, and the temple) was the religion of God's law and Pharisaic Judaism. Ezra the scribe, a returnee himself, becomes the prototype of the kind of religious expression that existed in the time of Jesus. As Bright says, "Here in the Exile there was already taking shape that form in which the faith of Israel was subsequently to express itself for centuries to come. . . . Israel was in transition from a nation with a national cult to the law community of Judaism."[10] If the apocalyptic, says Bright, "hoped for a Kingdom that only

7. Bright, *Kingdom of God*, 149.

8. Bright, *Kingdom of God*, 154.

9. Bright, *Kingdom of God*, 169.

10. Bright, *Kingdom of God*, 134.

God could produce, it might be said that the Holy Commonwealth [based on the keeping of the law] envisioned a Kingdom which man's righteousness could, if not produce, at least precipitate."[11] No longer was there an elect nation existing proudly. But there was the law that could be kept and the catastrophic intervention of God which could be hoped for. And as Bright notes, "The law . . . took over the function of prophecy: that of stating the Word of God." It became also, sadly, "the pathology of Judaism."[12]

Into this situation came John the Baptist, Jesus, and the apostles, proclaiming and inaugurating a new—at least from the perspective of their contemporaries—form of the kingdom.

The Church and the Kingdom

Jesus did not preach the church. Rather Jesus saw the church emerging out of the irruption of the kingdom and serving the kingdom.[13] That is, disciples of Jesus are "companions in the kingdom," as the disciple John said (Rev 1:9). The purpose of the church is not to "bring in the church" but to bring in the kingdom. As Charles Ringma, as mentioned above, stated about the relation of the kingdom to the church:

> The church birthed in the kingdom is to reflect the kingdom of God
> and to invite others into its embrace. In doing this the church is a
> *sign, servant and sacrament* of the kingdom of God. The church's
> fulfilment will be when it is fully consummated in the kingdom.[14]

So Jesus invited people not to join the church but to come under the gracious rule of God, in effect, to join God, to be part of the family of God (Father, Son, and Spirit) and to share in God's work and rule on earth and

---

11. Bright, *Kingdom of God*, 170.

12. Bright, *Kingdom of God*, 174–75.

13. Bright devotes a whole chapter to the kingdom and the church, 215–43. In it he says: "Jesus founded no ecclesiastical organization, not even of the truest sort, but as Messiah he came to call out the Remnant. In that true Israel which was obedient to his call lie the seeds of his Church, his *ekklesia* (i.e., the ones called out). . . . The New Testament church saw itself . . . as the people of that Kingdom, the 'eschatological community' which was already living in the age to come. It was, then, to busy itself in those last days between the Resurrection and the expected end in proclaiming the Kingdom in the entire world and in summoning men to its rule." Bright, *Kingdom of God*, 225, 232.

14. Email to the author, February 10, 2021, emphasis mine.

thereby be the people of God, the church.[15] But the complete identification of the church with the kingdom is not the only misunderstanding of the kingdom of God. The kingdom that Jesus announced and embodied is not just the best ideology or social enterprise human beings can conceive. It is the incursion of the new world, God's new world coming. And the final vision of the New Testament is the fulfilment of the kingdom. That vision is taken up in chapter 14 below, but, as we will see, there in the consummated kingdom believers will work (or rule) with Jesus for ever and ever.

So what is our part in bringing in the kingdom? As we will see, drawing on Ringma's statement, there are three in particular: witness, whereabouts, and work.

Announcing the Kingdom

First, the kingdom comes by witness. As Arias Mortimer says, "We are not sent to preach the church but to announce the kingdom."[16] So the first disciples were commissioned to preach that the kingdom had come near.[17] This news of the coming kingdom is like a seed to be received in good soil, which surely means responsive lives.[18] Philip found this good soil among the Samaritans.[19] Later the Apostle Paul tried to find that good soil as he argued persuasively about the kingdom in the Jewish synagogues,[20] though he later added speaking to Gentiles including people gathered in the Mars Hill forum in Athens for discussions and debates.[21] Summarizing his ministry, Paul told the Ephesians that he had preached the kingdom of God widely. Even when Paul was under house arrest in Rome, he explained the

15. Consider again the words of George Eldon Ladd. On one hand, Ladd says, "The kingdom of God is a miracle. It is an act of God. It is supernatural. Men cannot build the kingdom, they cannot erect it." But, on the other hand, Ladd notes, "[The disciples of the Lord] performed the signs of the kingdom (Luke 10:9, 17). . . . Thus the Kingdom of God was at work among men not only in the person of our Lord but also through his disciples as they brought the word and the signs of the Kingdom to the cities of Galilee." Ladd, *Gospel of the Kingdom*, 64, 115.

16. Arias, *Announcing the Reign of God*, 118.

17. Matt 10:7.

18. Matt 13:23.

19. Acts 8:12.

20. Acts 19:8.

21. Acts 17:16–34.

kingdom to the Jews. [22] And how does this message relate to Jesus? The keys to the kingdom are given to the person who confesses Jesus as Son of God.[23]

So all people of the Way—the earliest name given to Christians—are called to be witnesses. Where we have opportunity we can put in a good word for Jesus and the kingdom he is bringing. This witness is expressed both in word and deed, as was the case with Jesus and the early apostles who cared for whole persons, addressed the powers influencing people's lives, and demonstrated through signs the reality of the new world coming. Indeed this stunning witness in word and deed has brought human flourishing through the ages. It is simply untrue that "the church has never done the world any good."[24] And because this message is the long-standing purpose and action of God plus the people of God in history, kingdom teachers are instructed to bring out new treasures as well as old.[25] It is as old as Adam and as new as Jesus. It is what our neighbor needs. But there is more than witness involved in bringing in the kingdom.

Being Kingdom People Where We Are

Second, the kingdom comes by the whereabouts *of the people of faith.* The Quaker philosopher Elton Trueblood once said that "Church-goer is a vulgar ignorant word and should never be used. You *are* the church wherever you go."[26] The people of God are daily projected into the world in schools, workplaces, hospitals, governments, and neighborhoods. We are like seeds sown in soil, yeast folded into dough, light shining in darkness, salt seasoning meat, keys put into locks—all kingdom images of penetration. And there is one more Old Testament metaphor of kingdom penetration: we are like spies exploring the possibility of penetration. So the church cannot be photographed with a still camera. One needs a video, or even an angiogram, to capture the heart rhythm of blood gathering and dispersion in the human body. So then how does the kingdom come through the whereabouts of kingdom people?

22. Acts 20:25; 28:23–31.

23. Matt 16:19.

24. See the extraordinary volume tabulating what the people of God has done through history in good times and bad, Oliver, *Social Achievements of the Christian Church.*

25. Matt 13:52.

26. This was heard by the author in 1959 at McMaster University, when Trueblood was a guest lecturer.

The kingdom comes partly through a process like osmosis. Osmosis is defined as the

> spontaneous passage or diffusion of water or some other solvent through a semipermeable membrane. If a solution is separated from a pure solvent by a membrane that passes the solvent but not the solute, the solvent will go through the membrane, diluting the solution.[27]

Another way of saying this is that every one of us as kingdom people has an influence. Often we are unconscious of the effect our lifestyle, our words and actions, are having on those around us, but it is happening. People are watching, listening, and evaluating. We leave a mark, a stamp on people. Writing to Timothy, Paul said, "You . . . know all about my teaching, *my way of life*, my purpose, faith, patience, love, endurance, persecutions, sufferings" (2 Tim 3:10, emphasis mine). This happens in families, neighborhoods, workplaces, schools and universities, government offices, factories, social agencies, hospitals and medical clinics. The kingdom comes (partly) by osmosis. But there is more.

Working the Kingdom In

Third, the kingdom comes in part through human work.[28] Augustine, quoted above, in the fourth century, wrote, "God without us will not, as we without God cannot."[29] More recently New Testament scholar N. T. Wright has written: "[Christians] are not just to be a sign and foretaste of [the] ultimate salvation: they are to be *part* of the means by which God makes this happen in both the present and the future."[30] The emphasis in this sentence is on the word *part*. The reason why this is not a simple question has to do with the way Jesus taught about the rule and reign of God.

Do we autonomously bring in the kingdom through social programs, righteous business practices, environmental stewardship, and caring for the poor? No. Can the kingdom come without these? Yes and no. Yes, God is

27. Stevens, ed., *Webster's New Explorer Desk Encyclopedia*, 899.

28. For a full treatment of this subject see Witherington, *Work*. See also Stevens, *Other Six Days*, and *Work Matters*, chapters 17–20. For the development of work ethic and work perspective from the Greek philosophers to the present in the Western world, see Hardy, *Fabric of This World*.

29. Quoted in Sherman, *Kingdom Calling*, 238.

30. Wright, *Surprised by Hope*, 200.

able to bring in his new world without our human effort. No, it is usually a divine human partnership. We are "co-workers with God," as Paul cryptically says in 1 Corinthians 3:9. This is particularly evident in the final vision of the Bible, where believers "will reign [with God] forever and ever" (Rev 22:5). Read it this way: "We will work *with* God forever and ever." In this matter both biblical testaments witness to this co-creation or sub-creation of divine human partnership. Kingdom work advances and improves human life. It seeks to bring God's shalom into the world. It alleviates poverty. It welcomes God's life-giving rule in the world and in people (this brings about new birth and new life). There is a parable in Luke about this.

In the parable of the Ten Minas (Luke 19:11–27) Jesus was nearing Jerusalem and people thought that the kingdom of God was going to appear at once (v. 11). So he told the story of a person of noble birth who was going to a distant country to be appointed as king, during which absence he trusted ten of his servants with money equivalent to three months' wages.[31] But the trust was linked with a command: "Put this money to work until I come back" (v. 13). Interestingly, the Greek word for "put to work" (*pragmateusasthe*), sometimes translated "trade with," gives us the English word *pragmatic*. So be pragmatic with what you have been given—talents, abilities, gifts, and opportunities. Put it to work for the King and the kingdom. Some of the servants did this in spades, one making ten more, and another five. But the foolish person had his original one mina to show for his effort. He had stowed it and later presented it intact, with inauspicious results in the parable. He lost what he had. Use it or lose it. And the reason for his failure was unfounded fear of a bully master. So, be pragmatic. Invest in the kingdom. But is all good work kingdom work?

Work, as we have said, is kingdom work when it creates new wealth, alleviates poverty, brings well-being to people, embellishes and improves human life, as it engages powers resistant to God's coming *shalom*. Does all good work do this? No, not even all church work or missionary service. In this life all our work is a mixed bag, soiled and tainted with the long-standing effects of sin and disruption. But some of our work is part of that kingdom, will contribute to the breaking in of the kingdom and will outlast our own lifetimes in some way beyond our imagination. Paul notes in 1 Corinthians 15:58, "Your labor in the Lord is not in vain." Oh for the

31. There is actually a historical background to this parable. In 4 BC Archelaus went to Rome to be confirmed as king over Judea. At the same time a Jewish embassy of fifty people went to Rome to resist his appointment. The revenge inflicted by Archelaus when he returned would not have been forgotten. See Jeremias, *Parables of Jesus*, 59.

definitive way to unpack that brief pregnant phrase from the resurrection chapter! When, I ask, is our work "in the Lord"?

Certainly it is not the religious character of our work, the fact that the Bible is open and God's name is actually spoken, which makes it "in the Lord." Is it that the work was done with a different *motive*—out of love to God and neighbor? Or is it that the *method* of the work is in harmony with God's purposes and God's declared values—forgiveness, boundary-breaking behavior, transparency, extraordinary service, being just and fair, integrity of word and deed, and other salty values?[32] Or is it the *purpose* of the work that makes it "in the Lord" as it conforms to God's purpose of bringing human and creational flourishing? Or it is that the *goal* of the work is formed by the vision of God's final restoration and renewal of everything—people, peoples, communities, and creation itself? Certainly kingdom work is not merely religious work; but nor is it secular work. Dualism is dead. Kingdom work unifies everything we do in the home, marketplace, or educational institution into a sacrament, a means of bringing grace into the world and to people for the common good and that through down-to-earth work—the kingdom of God in working clothes.

All kinds of work can be kingdom work.

- *Service work*: Serving people directly, physically, emotionally, intellectually, socially, and spiritually—home care, public health care, counselling, teaching, barbering, caring professions, educators, homemaking —helping people flourish.

- *Culture work*: art, music, images, IT, communication, film, internet, media, system engineering.

- *Creational work*: earth keeping, farming, exploration.

---

32. Concerning salty kingdom values: *forgiveness and accountability*—giving people a second chance, going the second mile (Matt 18:21–35; 5:41); *integrity in word and deed*—letting your yes be yes, inner and outer life in sync, transparency (Matt 5:37); *fairness and justice*—doing the right thing in compensation, purity of product, handling of money; *extraordinary service*—going beyond duty (Col 4:1; Luke 17:7–10); *boundary-breaking behavior* (Luke 5:27–31); *stewardship*—treasuring the gifts of others, caring for creation, developing an empowering organizational culture (Matt 25:14–30); *empowerment*—releasing other people's gifts and talents, helping others to thrive in service (Eph 4:11–12); *shalom and being socially responsible*—neighbor love personally and socially (Matt 22:39); *joy*—experiencing a God-infusion of exuberance and well-being that is not dependent on circumstances—some have called this "fun" in the workplace (Phil 4:4). See Bakke, *Joy at Work*.

- *Social work:* creating community, facilitating communication, listening, building homes and workplaces and hospitals and schools, providing safety, and seeing that justice is done.

- *Powers work:* grappling with the principalities and powers: political, ecclesiastical, judicial structures, images, institutions, angels and demons, death, the demonic, dealing with unjust structures.

- *Spiritual work:* intercessory prayer, proclamation, spiritual direction, pastoral care, spiritual leadership.

All Ways of Contributing to the Kingdom of God . . . Now and Coming

So we must live, work, and witness with the ambiguity of the kingdom—it is here and not yet here; it is something we can participate in but we cannot bring it in by ourselves. John Bright asks, "Who will tell us that in escaping the tension of the Kingdom we have betrayed ourselves?" He continues:

> Yet is this plodding survival which lives at peace with the secular order, without tension and with no inkling of that Other Order which is ever intruding, less than that? Or is the Kingdom so small a thing that we can just take it by the arm and usher it in on our own terms, if only we would set our minds to do it? No, we cannot put the awful immediacy and the radical challenge of the Kingdom from our minds, nor turn it into a figure of speech, or perhaps a pale synonym for the sum total of human good, and remain the New Testament Church. For the New Testament Church is the people of the Kingdom of God.[33]

So there it is. God can do it without us. But mostly God chooses to do it with us. But we cannot do it without Godwardness, without dependence on God himself. Augustine had the right balance: "God without us will not, as we without God cannot."[34]

33. Bright, *Kingdom of God*, 242–43.
34. Quoted in Sherman, *Kingdom Calling*, 238.

6

The King in Working Clothes

"All authority in heaven and on earth has been given to me. Therefore go."

—Jesus in Matthew 28:18–19

"In love a throne will be established; in faithfulness a man will sit on it—one from the house of David."

—Isaiah 16:5

GOD THE WORKER BECAME a worker on earth—in person. Jesus the God-man was himself born into a working-class family. Today we would call him a "blue-collar worker." His father Joseph was undoubtedly a carpenter. And Jesus learned the trade from his father. As a carpenter myself I can understand how he banged his thumb, dropped a plank on his toe, cut his finger with a chisel and wiped it on his working clothes, dealt with an awkward customer, and lay in bed at night figuring out how to finish a job. He was God moved in with us, the Son of God, the Word became flesh who made his dwelling among us (John 1:14). So far as we can glean from the text, he worked from about fourteen years of age until thirty, seemingly supporting the family as we do not hear of his adopting father Joseph on the scene. Jesus knew what it was like to select wood, cut it, shape it, sand it, and make it into something useful, whether a crib, a table, or a custom-shaped ox yoke (Matt 11:28). He was possibly an entrepreneur since the Greek word, *tekton*, commonly translated as "carpenter," can mean someone who designs and builds a house or a boat. He did this day in and day out. And when he was baptized by John the Baptist and the Father spoke well of him—"I am well pleased with you"—he had not given a sermon or worked a miracle even though he knew the world was going to hell in a handbasket. The King was in working clothes.

Add to that the fact that of Jesus' 132 public appearances in the New Testament, 122 were in the marketplace. Of fifty-two parables Jesus told, forty-five had a workplace context. Of forty divine interventions recorded in Acts, thirty-nine were in the marketplace or the public square. Jesus called twelve normal working individuals, not clergy, to build his church—and some of them had questionable professions.[1] At thirty years of age he changed occupations and became an itinerant teacher, rabbi, and missionary. He died on a cross made by another carpenter who might also have been employed to make the sign over his head, "King of the Jews," and was raised from a tomb carved out of a rock by a mason. So it is not surprising that we started an Institute for Marketplace Transformation with the motto: work, worker, and workplace.[2] In this chapter we wish to see how Jesus himself is King of kings in active rule over work, worker, and the workplace. But, during his lifetime on earth, the kingship of Jesus was an enigmatic problem.

To explore that question I have chosen to unpack a pithy saying of the apostle Paul in Colossians: "Christ in you, the hope of glory" (Col 1:27), in a text which describes how Jesus is King, though the word is not used in the text.

Christ Is King in the Work

"Christ in you, the hope of glory."

First we must ask why some people are called Christians and why the faith is called Christianity. We ask this question because the Christian way believes that God is three-in-one: Father, Son, and Holy Spirit. The answer is stunning. Christ is the way we come to know God, and to know God in the intimate relations of Father, Son, and Spirit. "No one comes to the Father,"

---

1. I owe this summary to Allan Bussard, director of Integra in Bratislava, Slovakia.
2. See our website: https://imtglobal.org.

Jesus said, "except through me" (John 14:6). "Anyone who has seen me has seen the Father" (14:9).

Christ is the aperture through which the glory of God comes to us. "The Word became flesh and made his dwelling among us. We have seen his glory, the glory of the one and only Son, who came from the Father, full of grace and truth" (John 1:14). "Glory is beauty, goodness, and truth combined with power," says James Byran Smith in *The Magnificent Story*.[3] Glory takes us beyond the ordinary to the extraordinary. It is transcendent. So to the Colossians, Paul says: "Christ . . . the hope of glory." Here is the background to this saying.

For the Colossians Jesus was not considered to be enough in himself to bring people to God. The teaching they had received was this: You need Jesus *plus stuff*—stuff like religious ceremony, suppressing your body, putting down the physical, then you can really experience God. And Paul here says Jesus is enough. In chapter 1 he gives an amazing picture of Jesus as the Son of God (1:15–20): the Son is "the image of the invisible God" (Col 1:15). "God was pleased to have all his fullness dwell in him" (1:19). But when Paul turns to the work of Christ he says something truly magnificent.

Christ is **Creator**. "In him all things were created" (1:16). Yes, Jesus implemented the entire creation. In fact everything was created not only *by* him but *for* him. Because God invites his God-imaging creatures to enter his ongoing work this means that people who are artists, musicians, people in information technology, business people, and entrepreneurs are "doing the Lord's work." They are doing the King's work. The King has working clothes on in those who are creating new things.

He is also **Sustainer**. "In him all things hold together" (1:17). He is the glue of the universe. He keeps gravity going. Because God invites his God-imaging creatures to enter his ongoing work this means that people who are in systems engineering, management, homemaking, garbage collecting, policing, and those in politics are "doing the Lord's work," doing the King's work. The King has working clothes on in people who sustain life in the world.

But the Son is also **Redeemer**. He reconciled everything to himself, brought harmony into the world, brought people back into relationship with God, and brought about human flourishing, "making peace through his blood, shed in the cross" (Col 1:20), reconciling to himself not just people but even the powers, the invisible forces and personages and principles

3. Smith, *Magnificent Story*, 60.

of life that resist the kingdom of God and frustrate life for people (see Col 2:15). Because God invites his God-imaging creatures into his ongoing work this means that people who are technicians (fixing things), pastors, doctors, and counselors are "doing the Lord's work." They are doing the King's work. The King has working clothes on with people who are involved in correcting and redeeming things, as well as people and places.

But the Son revealed in Jesus is also **Consummator**. He is "the first-born from the dead" (1:18), the prototype of what and who we and all creation will become. And this is our hope of glory because Jesus is the first born and the first to be resurrected—pointing where everything is going. Christ is King of creation, King of the universe, King of redemption, and King of the glorious future. Christ the King is the hope of glory. Because God invites his God-imaging creatures into his ongoing work this means that people who are journalists (explaining where things are going), people working in the media, educators, pastors, and parents are "doing the Lord's work." They are doing the King's work. The King wears working clothes in the people who point to the future in their work. Lesslie Newbigin once said,

> [As a generation] we are without conviction about any worthwhile end to which the travail of history might lead. . . . The gospel is vastly more than an offer to men who care to accept it of a meaning for their personal lives. . . . And it has—what Marxism lacks—a faith regarding the final consummation of God's purpose in the power of which it is possible to find meaning for world history which does not make personal history meaningless, and meaning for personal history which does not make world history meaningless."[4]

The end, the new heaven and new earth is the kingdom fully come. In C. S. Lewis's children's chronicles it is called Narnia, Aslan's land. I resist the heading in Revelation 22 in the NIV "Eden Restored." The new heaven and new earth is not Eden restored but Eden on steroids. Yes, we can and should hold up this world and this life for oohs and ahhs.[5] But the Christ-future is much more magnificent.

---

4. Newbigin, *Honest Religion for Secular Man*, 42.

5. Capon, *An Offering of Uncles*, 163–64: "The work of theology in our day is not so much interpretation as contemplation: God and the world need to be held up for oohs and ahhs before they can be safely analysed."

"**Christ**, the hope of glory" brings perspective. Simply this: *our work in the world has dignity and meaning because we are entering into Christ's work and that work is kingdom work.* But now we must ask a second question. How do we relate to Christ the King? If our work is exalted by association with Christ's work, how do we get associated with Christ, and what does that mean for us as workers?

Christ the King in the Worker

"Christ in you, the hope of glory."

Years ago I bought a book written by a psychiatrist and a psychoanalyst, R. D. Laing. The book was entitled *The Politics of Experience and the Bird of Paradise*. It was written at the time when modernity was dying and just as postmodernity was emerging. But he was prophetic. He could see where things were going. He wrote:

> We are not satisfied with faith, in the sense of an implausible hypothesis irrationally held; we demand to experience the "evidence."
> . . . Having lost our experience of the spirit, we are expected to have faith. But this faith comes to be a belief in a reality that is not evident. There is a prophecy in Amos that there will be a time when there will be a famine in the land, "not a famine for bread, nor a thirst for water, but of hearing the words of the Lord." That time has now come to pass. It is the present age.[6]

"We demand to experience the evidence." This is something that faith in Jesus can wonderfully address, especially today. All of us who are engaged in giving a reason for the hope within us, commonly called apologetics, find that the rational proofs for the existence of God hold little weight especially today. So today we need to defend God, as someone said, the way we defend a lion, by letting it loose. People are looking for the proof of experience. And experience, it turns out, is one of the ways we know that something is true.

One of the gifts John Wesley left the church is the quadrilateral. This is the four ways we come to know something as true: Scripture, tradition (the teaching of the church through the centuries), reason, and experience.

6. Laing, *Politics of Experience and the Bird of Paradise*, 15, 118.

We are going to explore this last one now as we brood on the second word in Paul's concise and evocative sentence: "Christ *in* you the hope of glory."

What, after all, is the genius of being a Christian? It is not just the imitation of Christ, not just the worship of Christ, not just following the example of Christ, not just doing what Jesus taught, and not just doing what Jesus would do, as good as these things are. That was the problem in Colossae: Jesus *plus* stuff. You need to do this or that, punish your body, act religiously, do this or that practice. But the essence of the Christian experience is not that at all. The essence is that you are in Christ. "Christ in you the hope of glory."

Christ dwells in us and we dwell in Christ, which has led to Paul's cryptic, "I in Christ, Christ in me."[7] The Gospels are full of it, not just the letters. "I am the vine," said Jesus, "you are the branches. If you remain in me and I in you, you will bear much fruit" (John 15:5). It also appears in the letters of John: "That which we have heard, which we have seen with our eyes, which we have looked at and our hands have touched . . . this we proclaim to you . . . that you also may have fellowship with us. And *our fellowship is with the Father and with his Son, Jesus Christ*" (1 John 1:1–3, emphasis mine). The lights should flicker on at this point! New Testament scholar Adolf Deissmann calls this "Christ mysticism." Mysticism is direct contact with reality that is beyond ourselves. It is personal engagement. Deissmann notes how in the world of the apostle Paul there were mystery religions that promised *union mysticism*, namely, that you become one with the god of your choice and your identity is lost. Your personality was merged with the person of the god. I sometimes hear Christians say something like that. "Make me nothing. You be everything." This is like a drop of water plunged into the ocean, losing oneself in the great sea of ultimate reality. But that is *not* the Christian experience. The Christian experience, as Deissmann proposes, is *communion mysticism*. Communion mysticism is the sanctification of the personality through the presence of Christ. Deissmann puts it this way: "Christ-intimacy was experience and confirmation of Christ-intimacy. . . . [Paul did not] become Christ . . . he was one whom Christ possessed and a Christ-bearer."[8]

Theologian Thomas Torrance put it this way:

> The doctrine of the Trinity is the central dogma of Christian theology, the fundamental grammar of our knowledge of God. Why?

7. See Gal 2:20; 2 Cor 12:2; John 15:4.

8. Deissmann, *Paul*, 150–56.

Because the doctrine of the Trinity gives expression to the fact
that . . . God draws near to us in such a way as to draw us near to
himself within the circle of his knowing of himself.[9]

Thus we become co-lovers of God, co-lovers of the world, co-lovers of
people—drawn into the love life of the triune God. We are not just imita-
tors, not just people who try to obey the teaching, and not just followers.
We have fellowship with the King. We know the King in the sense of that
word in the original language, namely, we have intercourse with the King.
This is something that the beautiful Greek word *perichoresis* expresses. I in
Christ; Christ in me, or as Paul says, "Christ in you, the hope of glory." Yes,
we can experience the evidence. And there is hope of glory in this.

In the words of Paul in 2 Corinthians 3, we become increasingly glorified as we look to the Lord and the Spirit works in us. "And we all, who with
unveiled faces contemplate the Lord's glory, are being transformed into his
image with ever-increasing glory, which comes from the Lord, who is the
Spirit" (2 Cor 3:18). We are not, Paul says here, like Moses who had to
wear a veil when he came out of the tabernacle *because the glow was going
to fade*. But, in contrast there is progressive glorification. In the words of 2
Peter 1:4, we "partake of [or participate in] the divine nature." It is called
theosis—becoming Godlike. We are transfigured. Thomas Dubay says, "We
have been created and redeemed for the eternal ecstasy of an interpersonal
immersion in the triune God, seeing infinite Beauty face to face."[10] How
does this affect the worker in the kingdom of God?

What happens with Christ mysticism is that we gain the mind, attitude, and values of Christ. In becoming a Christ-person we are justified
by faith, that is, we are declared not guilty by virtue of our identification
with Christ and his saving work on the cross. But justification is not only
imputed to us. It is *imparted* to us through communion with Christ. So,
gradually—and it is a process—our values become the values of Christ and
we become better in relationship to our work, our colleagues, our boss,
our employees, and even our enemies. *So not only has our work been given
dignity and meaning through Christ but we as workers are being transformed.
We have a changed motivation. As Paul says twice in Colossians chapter three,
"it is the Lord Christ you are serving" (Col 3:23–24). We work simultaneously
for and in Christ.*

Thirdly, the King's way of life affects even the workplace.

9. Torrance, *Trinitarian Perspectives*, 1.

10. Quoted in Smith, *Magnificent Story*, 125.

Christ the King in the Workplace

"Christ in you, the hope of glory."

Here is the context of Paul's pithy statement that Christ in you is the hope of glory. In Colossians Paul says that he has become the church's servant

> by the commission God gave me to present to you the Word of God in its fullness—the mystery that has been kept hidden for ages and generations, but is now disclosed to the Lord's people. To them God has chosen to make known among the Gentiles the glorious riches of this mystery, which is Christ in you, the hope of glory. He is the one we proclaim, admonishing and teaching everyone with all wisdom, so that we may present everyone fully mature in Christ. To this end I strenuously contend with all the energy Christ so powerfully works in me (Col 1:25–28).

This is the full gospel. The mystery is now revealed, that Jew and Gentile, bond and free, male and female, all kinds and classes of people can be connected with Christ the King and share in the inbreaking of his kingdom. This is not just Christ in your soul and not just Christ in your spirit. "You" means the whole person. You get saved, not just your soul. And not just you but what you do: work, leisure, relationships, money, sexuality, friendships, citizenship. And it is not just you that gets transformed but also workplaces.

What is the gospel of Jesus? As I have said, Jesus did not preach the gospel of soul salvation. He preached the "gospel of the kingdom of God" (Matt 4:17; 24:14). In Colossians Paul spells this out in terms of the realities of everyday work and family. The kingdom is coming now (partly) and in the future fully. It is the rule of God through which people can experience shalom and flourish. Work and relationships can be transformed, and people can live a fully human life. This is partially true for now but because of the resurrection of Christ we will ultimately be fully human in the new heaven and new earth. It is more than soul salvation. It is more than religious activity and practices. It is more than subduing the body. It is more than knowing you are loved by God. It is more than having your sins forgiven. It is life, abundant life, flourishing life. It is the hope of glory.

So the gospel of the kingdom is the end of dualism. Dualism is perhaps the most pernicious heresy in the Christian church worldwide. Dualism says that the body is bad but the spirit or soul is good. Paul does not mean this when he says to set our minds on things above, not on earthly things

(Col 3:1–2).[11] Dualism was smashed by Jesus. Marianne Meye Thompson in her commentary on Colossians says, "But there is no dualism here between heavenly and earthly, as though to set one's mind on 'the things that are above' implies a spirituality uninterested in the world created in and for Christ."[12] The essence of the gospel is that it leads to flourishing life, not religion, not upper life as opposed to lower life. "You have been brought to fullness," Paul affirms in Colossians 2:10.[13] The Colossian teaching Paul corrected was a set of beliefs based on certain rules and regulations that promised a deeper spiritual experience. This involved certain feasts, festivals (new moons or Sabbaths), holy days and fasting, self-denial, abstention from certain foods, and even harsh treatment of the body. Through this you would supposedly get higher levels and understandings of the mysteries of Christ.

Subduing the body is wrong in *perspective*—it does not grasp the significance of the resurrection of the body or the resurrection of Jesus. The body is holy. It is wrong in *practice*, in that once the practice is stopped the old drive reappears, usually with greater vigor (see also Col 2:23). Humiliation of the physical flesh does not lead to humility but pride, being puffed up.[14] So, and this is great news, God redeems the entirety of our embodied life.

In the kingdom of God there is no dualism between heavenly and earthly, no dualism between human life in Christ (work, relationships etc.) and specific activities in the people of God (such as stated Christian service and activities). Thompson says, "heavenly-mindedness transforms every part of life by seeing it in relation to the exalted Christ."[15]

In Colossians 3 Paul says the relationship of slave and master is not dominance and compliance but service and service. That transforms the

11. See Thompson, *Colossians and Philemon*, 71. "To 'set one's mind on the things that are above' does not mean to 'think about heaven,' but to orient one's life and devotion to God rather than to self or the world. Athanasius once described the human plight as a misdirection of the senses. Human beings 'have turned their eyes not longer upward but downward'; they 'were seeking about God in nature and in the world of sense, feigning gods for themselves.'"

12. Thompson, *Colossians and Philemon*, 71. "But there is no dualism here between heavenly and earthly, as though to set one's mind on 'the things that are above' implies a spirituality uninterested in the world created in and for Christ." Dualism will be more completely expounded on in the next chapter.

13. Thompson, *Colossians and Philemon*, 7, 44, 65.

14. Thompson, *Colossians and Philemon*, 66.

15. Thompson, *Colossians and Philemon*, 72.

workplace. Instead of *over*powering one another we *em*power one another. And that is glory. Thought life—glory. Working life—glory. Relational life—glory. How can this be? Paul's answer is "in the Lord" (3:18, 20); "for the Lord" (3:23); "serving the Lord" (3:24); and because we have a "master (lord or king) in heaven" (4:1). Glory in all of life. Glory in all of life to come. There is life after life after death, as N. T. Wright puts it. And returning to our Colossians text which centers this chapter, we might put it graphically:

> "**Christ** in you, the hope of glory." Christ is king in work.
> "Christ **in** you, the hope of glory." Christ is king in the worker.
> "Christ in **you**, the hope of glory." Christ is king in the workplace.

And how does this Christ-communion happen?

Simone Weil was a Jewess who became a Christian but never joined the formal church, though she experienced the believing community in the two or three gathered. She wrote,

> Over the infinity of space and time, the infinitely more infinite love of God comes to possess us. He comes at his own time. We have the power to consent to receive him or to refuse. If we remain deaf he comes back again and again like a beggar. . . . We have only not to regret the consent we gave him, the nuptial yes.[16]

If the revelation of Christ is a divine gift, the great challenge of evangelism is how to make the self-revelation of Christ happen. So to Peter, who confessed that Jesus was the Christ, Jesus said, "this was not revealed to you by flesh and blood, but by my Father in heaven" (Matt 16:17), Jesus implicitly raises this critical question: How does this actually happen? Do we invite ourselves into the Trinity? Does the Trinity, and in particular Jesus, invite us into fellowship with him? And are there conditions, such as being real, being true to ourselves, and admitting our need? Does God wait for our invitation or do we wait for his? This is certainly mysterious. Our puny minds cannot fully take it in. But this is for sure: If you hear him knocking at the door of your heart as a worker, in your work, and in your workplace you welcome him. And he will come in.

16. Weil, *Waiting on God*, 91–92.

PART THREE

Kingdom Values and Virtues in the Marketplace

7

Three Kingdom Values to Die For

EVERY GOOD BUSINESS HAS a value statement, often in public view to customers and clients. Churches do the same, as well as not-for-profits. Such statements are important. Values are cherished ways of behavior. They motivate us and give us direction. I hope that you will not only embrace the three values outlined in this chapter, but that they may become embedded in your person as virtues.[1] These three primary values were adopted by a yearlong process with the board and fellows group of the Institute for Marketplace Transformation. Incidentally they spell out the acronym IMT: integrating, meaning, and thriving. They are kingdom values that apply to work, workers, and the workplace.

Integrating

"When your eyes are healthy [single], your whole body also is full of light. . . . See to it, then, that the light within you is not darkness."

—LUKE 11:34–35

To cherish the value of integrating means adopting behavior and thinking that brings things together under the purpose and presence of God—to see everything as sacred and God-given. Satan is a professor of *dis*integration

1. For a reflection on the relationship of values and virtues see Benson, "Virtues" and "Values."

and is the founder of dualism (Gen 3:1–5). The Lord Jesus is the professor of integration. Strangely, the original meaning of the word *religion* means "to bind together," binding things together into a rich seamless whole, or to use a biblical term, finding *shalom*. In Ephesians this wholeness or integration means bringing everything together into one under the headship of Christ (Eph 1:10). This means not separating our devotion to God and God's kingdom from everyday matters such as handling money, working in an enterprise, and making things. It destroys dualism.

Dualism says that the body is bad but the spirit or soul is good.[2] Dualism maintains that work in the world is secular and unholy, but church ministry, church worship, teaching Sunday school, and sharing the gospel is holy. Dualism suggests that the things of this life are unholy while the life we will live in the new heaven and new earth is holy. Dualism creates a hierarchy of occupations with respect to pleasing God (with missionary and pastor at the top and the stock broker near the bottom). Dualism gets expressed in religiosity and/or secularization when true Christian faith is *neither*.

Behind integration is a crucial truth, often missed in the reading of the early chapters of Genesis. God made this world as a temple for the presence and purpose of God. And God set in the middle of this temple-world (or, if you wish, this sanctuary-world) an image of God, in this case a creature that would represent himself, male and female—in God's image. Everything was *originally created sacred*. Since sin has marred everything now, today things are *either sacred or desecrated. But that means that nothing is secular*. What was once one and whole has become divided and separated. Simply put, this is the problem of dualism.[3]

Dualism exalts certain actions, some persons and some experiences, as divine. Indeed, the title *Reverend* is usually assigned to an ordained pastor while the term means to be held in reverence, something to be reserved for God. It is a pre-Christian designation. In the biblical theology of the whole people of God there are no "laypersons" in the usual sense—second class, untrained, unqualified, or secular. The two Greek words that could mean "layperson"—*laikoi* and *idiotes*—are never used by an inspired apostle to describe a Christian, while the term in Greek that gives us the English

2. Thompson, *Colossians and Philemon*, 71. "But there is no dualism here between heavenly and earthly, as though to set one's mind on 'the things that are above' implies a spirituality uninterested in the world created in and for Christ."

3. For an outline of the process by which dualism has infected the world, see Stevens and Lim, *Money Matters*, 42–54.

word *clergy* (*kleros*)—empowered, ordained, commissioned—is never used in Scripture exclusively for church leaders doing "holy things." Indeed the term is used for the whole people of God. That dignified people is expressed by the Greek word *laos* (which word does not mean "laity" but rather "the people of God"). So as companions in the kingdom we are in the ironic situation of being a people with no laypersons in the usual sense of that word and yet a people full of clergy in the true meaning of that word.

So integration as a Christian task, an apostolic mission, and a divinely given mandate to find everything in all creation unified under Christ, is simply to *live and work sacramentally*. Since that term usually refers to the Eucharist and baptism, and possibly more sacraments, these being grace mediated through material realities, it is important to affirm that if we truly integrate we will find God in everyday things; we will meet God and find grace and the meeting of heaven and earth in the everydayness of work, worker, and workplace.

In the history of the church there have been two ways in which this meeting of heaven and earth, this reintegration of things, has been proposed. The best of the "sacramental" traditions of the church have argued that there are special priests and sacred motions designated for handling the physical matter (bread and wine and water) *so that the people will become a universal priesthood and see all of life as an irruption of the kingdom, a sacramental expression of the grace of God.* This is expressed ably by N. T. Wright:

> A church that is learning the habits of the royal priesthood will celebrate the sacraments—those occasions when the life of heaven intersects mysteriously with the life of earth, not so that earth can control or manipulate heaven (that would be magic, not faith) but *so that the story of heaven may become concrete, physical reality within the life of earth.*[4]

Meanwhile the Quakers, with no priesthood and no stated sacraments take this stand because they wish to affirm that all the "common ventures of life" are sacramental, as Elton Trueblood puts it in his book by that title.[5]

Thus we can begin to live and work sacramentally. I say "begin" because this is a lifelong and history-long process just as the kingdom of God, which is the master integrating concept of Jesus, is both here now but coming in fullness at the end when Christ returns.

4. Wright, *After You Believe*, 223, emphasis mine.
5. Trueblood, *Common Ventures of Life.*

Speaking of rediscovering the sacramental nature of everyday life, Alexander Schmemann, an Orthodox theologian, takes us back to God's original intention in the garden.

> In the biblical story of creation man is presented . . . as a hungry being, and the whole world his food. . . . The "original" sin is not primarily that man has disobeyed God; the sin is that he ceased to be hungry for Him and for Him alone, ceased to see his whole life depending on the whole world *as a sacrament of communion with God.* The sin was not that he neglected his religious duties. *The sin was that he thought of God in terms of religion, i.e. opposing Him to life.* The only real fall of man is his noneucharistic life in a noneucharistic world.[6]

So integrating will be a process for us, never completed in our lifetime, but nevertheless very life-giving. David Sayson, formerly president of IMT, summarizes this process: Our role as image bearers is to mediate God's blessing to the rest of creation. The mode of integrating is as royal priests who bridge heaven and earth. The ultimate form of integrating faith and work is liturgy: work that is worship (which is the meaning of the Greek word *leitourgia*, which literally means "work for the people," a literal translation of the two words "*litos ergos*" or "public service" or "sacred service.")[7]

Through integrating we find meaning in our life and work.

Meaning

"The fear of the Lord [affectionate reverence for God] is the beginning of wisdom."

—PROVERBS 1:7

It has been said that while integrating and thriving (the third value) are behaviors, meaning is not a behavior. But is that true? Or is it a shrewd observation? In fact we do not discover meaning buried implicitly in our actions, works, enterprises, or ministries. *We bring meaning to them ourselves*

---

6. Schmemann, *For the Life of the World*, 11, 18, emphasis mine. Please note that *Eucharist* is the Greek word for "thanksgiving," though the term has become synonymous with Communion or the Lord's Supper.

7. Sayson, "Church Fathers and IMT."

or, conversely, meaning is attributed by other people. *Meaning* is a noun rather than a verb or participle, but the noun conveys "what is intended," "a significant quality," "implication of a hidden or special significance," and discovery of "purpose" (Webster). It can be argued that the whole purpose of the theological task is to discover the meaning of things. This includes the meaning of human life, human enterprise, history, and the kingdom of God. So while the noun *meaning* does not indicate where the significance comes from, we may need to use terms such as *deep meaning* or *divine meaning* or *sacred meaning* or *biblical meaning* to get at this value.

While we do not discover the deep-rooted and God-communicated meaning simply by doing something, such as crafting a table, or making a meal or a deal, we can discover the meaning and significance of that task by seeing how it relates to the purpose of God for humankind, how we are made like God to work and to do so in community and for others. We can discover this work is a practical way of loving our brother, sister, and neighbor, how to fulfill longings in ourselves for expression of giftedness and talents, and how it edifies the commonwealth, the larger community. Included in this list is quite naturally and significantly that through work we are able to provide for ourselves and loved ones. But in his *Whole New Mind*, Daniel Pink maintains that "meaning is the new money."[8] He quotes Victor Frankl, who writing a half-century earlier said, "People have enough to live, but nothing to live for; they have the means but no meaning."[9] We are incentivized, motivated, and empowered primarily by meaning. Without it we die—which is why so many people leave what they regard as relatively meaningless work in business to engage in ministry. Why? Because meaning has been brought to that work in the church, wrongly in my view, by the community of faith which has neglected bringing meaning to other human endeavors. Without meaning we are the walking dead.

Meaninglessness is abundantly found in society, in the media, and in general life. And one of the great things that the good news of the kingdom of God brings is meaningfulness. We are saved, among other things, from meaninglessness. That surprisingly is the under-the-surface message of the enigmatic book of Ecclesiastes. As a successful person this Solomon-like man surveys his own achievements "under the sun," that is, without reference to a transcendent God, and concludes with these words: "Yet when I surveyed all that my hands had done and what I had toiled to achieve,

8. Pink, *Whole New Mind*, 61.

9. Quoted in Pink, *Whole New Mind*, 218.

everything was meaningless, a chasing after the wind; nothing was gained under the sun" (Eccl 2:11). He does, however, at the end of his journey through meaninglessness come to a stunning conclusion: meaning is found with those who "fear God" (12:13)—"fearing" in the sense of reverent affection for God.

So what is the meaning that we seek to bring to work, worker, and workplace? It is simply this: we live, work, relate, envision, and create *for the glory of God and the good of the commonwealth.* Jesus put it this way in the two great commandments: to love God with all our heart, mind, soul, and strength and to love our neighbor as ourselves (Luke 10:27). Put differently, the meaning we wish to bring to work, worker, and workplace is that we *live and work in line with our Creator's purpose and presence and to benefit humankind and all creation.*

If the first value—integrating—concerns the worker and the second value—meaning—concerns the work, the third, thriving, concerns the workplace.

Thriving

"The fear of the Lord is a fountain of life."

—PROVERBS 14:27

"The tent of the upright will flourish."

—PROVERBS 14:11

As a behavior, thriving is not simply an action about which we could say, "Today I am going to thrive, not merely survive." To thrive is not merely to make a life goal to be successful, rich, famous, or even blessed, and then to take steps to get there using smart goals. It is not attained by self-help disciplines such as posited by the human potential movement with its oddly oxymoronic phrase, "human transcendence," as though we could transcend our humanity. But, unquestionably, thriving is something God wants for his creatures. Proverbs 14:11, noted above, maintains that "the tent of the upright will flourish."

This is displayed so brilliantly when Jesus came to his old home synagogue. After reading Isaiah 61 about bringing sight to the blind, good news to the poor, release of those in captivity, and helping people to find favor with God, he simply said, "That is me. I came to embody, announce and implement the reign of God by which human beings will flourish" (Luke 4:16–30). The story does not end there. When he went on to explain how this would come, especially that the flourishing kingdom would include outsiders, alienated people, and the rejected, they tried to kill him. So thriving has some countercultural dimensions. It is the inversion of some human longings.

As we discovered in chapter 1, the biblical vision of human thriving includes economic, social, emotional, creational, relational, and spiritual well-being (Luke 4:18–19). But this is not something we can summon up, or take a crash course on "how to thrive." It is given in the context of a divine-human dialogue, a gracious conspiracy, a co-creating enterprise. So what does it mean to thrive?

The church father Irenaeus (130–202 AD) famously said, "the glory of God is a living human being."[10] And this comes through an association with and a dependence on God. But this turns out to be—for those of us wanting to be fully alive—a death and resurrection. This involves turning from autonomy to dependence on God, being rooted in and dwelling in God. In truth we will ultimately thrive when in our resurrected life in the new heaven and new earth, we have become fully human in a way not experienced in this mortal life. But in this life, this partial thriving (when compared with the ultimate destiny) is obtained by a surprisingly negative and positive movement, called by ancient spiritual directors "mortification and aspiration." In Scripture it is described as crucifying the flesh (not the physical body but life lived outside of Christ and turned in on oneself) and walking in and keeping in step with the Spirit. So we are inundated with the fruit of the Spirit (Gal 5:16–26). The other biblical phrase for entering kingdom thriving is repentance, the very thing Jesus said in his first sermon in the Gospel of Matthew: "Repent, for the kingdom of heaven has come near [or is within your grasp]" (Matt 4:17). And what does it mean to repent?

Repentance is not just remorse—feeling badly about what we have done. Judas killed himself in remorse but never repented (Matt 27:3–5). Repentance is actually turning around, making an about-face, turning from darkness to light, from barely being alive to being born again, from being autonomous (your own god) to letting God be God, from orientation towards self to God-orientation, from pessimism and negativism toward the world and what is happening to embracing hope in the coming kingdom,

10. As quoted in Behr, *Becoming Human*, 1.

from taking our priorities, our values, our life purposes from the surrounding culture to embracing the values and priorities of the kingdom of God. Repentance means turning from loving self as the center of the universe to loving God with all our heart, soul, strength, and mind. Repentance means turning from the darkness of consumerism and soul-destroying images to the light of embracing an extravagant and joyful life.

While I was an undergraduate student at McMaster University, my pastor spoke one day in the university chapel. He simply read the text of Matthew 4:17 where Jesus says, "Repent for the kingdom of heaven is at hand." Before he sat down he said, "You don't want to repent, do you? But you will when you meet Jesus."

Jesus said that he came that we may "have life, and have it to the full" (John 10:10). He said that if we abide in him we will "bear much fruit" (read "thrive," John 15:5). And what does that look like? Here is what it looks like: *fruitfulness; productivity; joy and enjoyment; some personal fulfillment; meaningfulness; agency (making a difference like Adam in the garden); being empowered by a calling or divine purpose of our lives; being blessed.*[11] Ironically we discover in the Beatitudes, the subject of the next chapter, a surprising statement of thriving in the kingdom of God, that is, living and working in sync with God's new world coming. This comes through being poor in spirit, merciful, pure in heart, being hungry for righteousness, making peace and experiencing trouble (Matt 5:3–12).[12]

So in summary, integrating focuses on the *worker*—providing a wholistic and faith-full way of being in the world. Meaning is centered on the *work*—seeing the significance and value of what we are doing in the light of God's purpose and grace. Thriving points to the *workplace*—developing an environment and organizational culture in which people will flourish.

We pray that these three values will become ingrained in our characters and expressed in our behaviors. But it comes with the gospel invitation to repent and enter the kingdom of God. It is really a death and resurrection experience, which will become a lifelong process of continuous conversion. So embracing these values is an evangelical invitation: come to Jesus, embrace his death and resurrection, find full and abundant life in

11. See Banks, "Blessing," and Miller, "Success."

12. On human flourishing briefly, read Pennington, "Human Flourishing and the Bible." A more comprehensive approach is taken by Pennington in *Sermon on the Mount and Human Flourishing*.

him and you will be able to work for Jesus, find meaning in your life and work, to flourish now and forever. But not without a lot of trouble, as the next chapter will indicate.

8

Paradoxical Kingdom Virtues

The Beatitudes and the Marketplace

"The word of the Beatitudes . . . overturns our ideas and projects, reverses the obvious, thwarts our desires, and bewilders us, leaving us poor and naked before God."

—Servais Pinckaers[1]

"Jesus himself is the incarnation of the Beatitudes. Lived and proclaimed by Him, they become the spiritual values of a kingdom that is primarily Jesus himself."

—Segundo Galilea[2]

I DARE SAY THERE is hardly a human being alive in his or her right mind who does not want to be blessed and to flourish. Indeed, the pursuit of happiness is a fundamental theme of all philosophy and of every religion. In one of the strangest teachings of Jesus, included in what is called the Sermon on the Mount (Matt 5–7), we have an answer for the search for happiness. For good reason a famous and popular preacher called the Beatitudes "The Be Happy Attitudes." But there is more to the Beatitudes than a program of making yourself happy. In fact Jesus was talking about life

1. Quoted in Pennington, *Sermon on the Mount and Human Flourishing*, 154.
2. Quoted in Alexander and Brown, eds., *To Whom Shall We Go?*, xvi.

in the kingdom of God. And the kingdom starts now. The first and last Beatitude say "For theirs is the kingdom of God [or heaven]" (5:3, 10). But here is a curious thing.

What the Beatitudes Are Not and What They Are

The Beatitudes do not say what you have to do *in order to get into the kingdom*. For example, it is not saying if you want to inherit the earth you need to be meek. Or if you want to be called "children of God," you need to comport yourself as a peacemaker.[3] These are not entrance requirements to the kingdom. They describe what it is like when you *are* in the kingdom. Further, the Beatitudes are *not statements exclusively about a future kingdom period* when Christ returns and establishes his kingdom on earth. It is now—especially the first and last Beatitudes—and also in the future (that is the mystery). Finally, they are *not descriptions of eight different kinds of people*—they could all be the same person. What are they?

They are *encouragements* to recognize the kingdom in people around you and to recognize that you are in the kingdom. They are *declarations* of what it is really like to be a Christian. They are *congratulations* to disciples for the paradoxical goodness (flourishing) of being in the kingdom. They are *pictures* of "what the state of true God-centered human flourishing looks like," as Jonathan Pennington notes.[4] But if the Beatitudes are about "blessing," just what does it mean to be "blessed"?

The English word *blessed* comes from the Latin *beatus*, which means happy, blissful, fortunate, or flourishing. But the Greek word that is used to translate *beatus*, the word *makarios*, is not so accurately translated in English as "blessed," since "blessed" describes God's authoritative declaration of divine favor. *Makarios* ascribes happiness or flourishing to a particular person or state, which may be the result of God's blessing, but *that is not what it is expressing*. It is expressing the kingdom of God, and what a person experiences in the kingdom—this amazing, as we will see, upside-down kingdom.[5] So as Pennington says, "The Beatitudes [are] Jesus' answer to the

---

3. The relationship of the first part of the Beatitude to the second is very complicated and made more difficult by translation from the original Greek. See Pennington, *Sermon on the Mount and Human Flourishing*, 62–67.

4. Pennington, *Sermon on the Mount and Human Flourishing*, 47.

5. Pennington argues that the Greek is wrongly translated "blessed," which is a translation of the Hebrew word *barak*—God's authoritative declaration of divine favor,

great human question of happiness."[6] So it is about happiness in the largest sense, about thriving, flourishing, not just circumstantially feeling positive. The Beatitudes are *pictures* of "what the state of true God-centered human flourishing looks like," as Pennington notes.[7] Darrell Johnston translates the first one—"Blessed are the poor in spirit"—"You lucky bums! You blessed paupers!"[8] If that does not draw out the paradoxical nature of these kingdom signs then nothing can. So let's restate the Beatitudes in the light of the above:

- Flourishing are the poor in spirit because the kingdom of heaven is theirs.

- Flourishing are the mourners because they will be comforted.

- Flourishing are the humble/the meek because they will inherit the world.

- Flourishing are the ones hungering and thirsting for righteousness because they will be satisfied.

- Flourishing are the merciful because they will be given mercy.

- Flourishing are the pure in heart because they will see God.

- Flourishing are the peacemakers because they will be called the children of God.

- Flourishing are the ones persecuted on account of righteousness because the kingdom of heaven is theirs.

No question: the Beatitudes are paradoxical. You are really wealthy when you are poor or poor in spirit.[9] You are comforted when you are mourning. You inherit the earth when you are meek and humble. You are

---

effectual speech. Meanwhile the Hebrew word that comes closest to *makarios* is the Hebrew word *asre* (used in Psalm 1), not the Hebrew word for "blessing" (*barak*, from God—which is covenantal language). In the Greek version of the Old Testament *makarios* always translates *asre*. So, says Pennington, "Proclaiming an asherism [*asre*] or macarism is to make a value statement upon another member of the community, sage, or teacher and pronounce the subject(s) 'honorable'" (Pennington, *Sermon on the Mount and Human Flourishing*, 49).

6. Pennington, *Sermon on the Mount and Human Flourishing*, 61.

7. Pennington, *Sermon on the Mount and Human Flourishing*, 47.

8. Johnson, *Beatitudes*, 42.

9. Luke simply says "poor" not "poor in spirit." "Blessed are you who are poor, for yours is the kingdom of God" (Luke 6:20).

satisfied when you are hungry. You receive mercy when you give it. You see God when you are pure in heart. You are called children of God when you make peace. You are flourishing when you are facing terrible opposition. Servais Pinckaers, mentioned above, shows this paradoxical quality starkly.

> The word of the beatitudes penetrates us with the power of the Holy Spirit in order to break up our interior soil. It cuts through us with the sharp edge of trials and with the struggles it provokes. It overturns our ideas and projects, reverses the obvious, thwarts our desires, and bewilders us, leaving us poor and naked before God. All this, in order to prepare a place within us for the seed of new life.[10]

Signs of Kingdom Flourishing

So what are the signs that people have the virtues of the kingdom of God?

Sign One: **Right Self-Assessment**. Poor people are always dependent. And the poor in spirit are people who know they are needy. You are really flourishing, Jesus says, when you recognize that you have nothing to give, nothing to bring to God to merit acceptance and membership in God's family. It is a great thing to be spiritually bankrupt, like Peter when he met Jesus and said, "Away from me Jesus, I am a sinful man." Congratulations! You have everything in the kingdom of God, God's new world coming. Kingdom people in the marketplace are not the center of the universe and they know it. They don't know everything and are not all-sufficient.

Sign Two: **Experiencing Right Passion**. "Mourning" means you feel deeply the pain of the world, about what is going on, what is happening. You have God's heart like the prophets of old who had *orthopathy*, that is their hearts were lined up with God's heart. *Ortho* means straight and *pathos* means passion. They feel as God feels. And, guess what, they are flourishing when they have that passion. They will be comforted. The kingdom is coming. Kingdom people in the marketplace have passion for the right things. Indeed, one of the worst things would to be apathetic and simply not to care.

Sign Three: **Being Humble**. "Meekness" means one is not overpowering but submissive to authority. But meekness is not weakness. Two of the greatest leaders in the world were declared meek: Moses and Jesus! Indeed

---

10. Quoted in Pennington, *Sermon on the Mount and Human Flourishing*, 154.

the meekest of all, Jesus, will, along with his companions in the kingdom (Rev 1:9), inherit the earth (Rev 11:15). Psalm 37:11 says that very thing. Meekness means submissiveness under provocation, willingness to suffer rather than inflict injury. Meek people are not proud. Like the divine qualifications for the Old Testament king, they do not regard themselves "as better than their fellows" (Deut 17:20).[11] Surprisingly to some, the meek do inherit the earth! John Dickson summarizes some of the social science research on management in *Humilitas: A Lost Key to Life, Love, and Leadership*. Dickson defines humility as follows: "Humility is *the noble choice to forgo your status, deploy your resources or use your influence for the good of others before yourself.* More simply, you could say the humble person is marked by *a willingness to hold power in service of others.*"[12] In contrast to empires built on greed and dominating power that are eaten up, the kingdom built on meekness lasts forever.

Sign Four: ***Having Holy Desires***. Being "hungry and thirsty for righteousness" means being passionate for right relationships with God, other people, our inner selves, and creation. There are two kinds of righteousness: first by imputation—in Christ you are declared or imputed to be righteous—in virtue of your faith (2 Cor 5:21) and, second, by impartation—as we grow in Christlikeness (2 Cor 3:18; Col 1:27). Peter Kreeft remarks: "Dissatisfaction is the second best thing there is, because it dissolves the glue that entraps up to false satisfactions, and drives us to God, the only true satisfaction."[13] Yes, longingness is a great thing in the marketplace. It is a passion for growth and improvement, an unsettledness with the status quo. Good news: satisfaction is coming. Indeed it is here with Christ and Christ's kingdom. And the fact that you hunger for this is a sign you are in the right-side-up kingdom!

Sign Five: ***Being Softhearted***. Being "merciful" is not giving people what they deserve. The Greek word used here, *eleemones,* means love and kindness for those in misery and having a forgiving spirit, born personally of the experience of God's mercy. It is the kind of thing we see in the Gospels in the parables of the Good Samaritan and the Prodigal Son.[14] It is doing so from the gut or heart. If we do not practice mercy to others and yet wish it for ourselves we are not really asking for mercy. Is it possible to

11. See the requirements for the king in Deuteronomy 17:14–20, especially verse 20.

12. Quoted in Alexander and Brown, eds., *To Whom Shall We Go?*, 31.

13. Johnson, *Beatitudes*, 83.

14. Luke 10:25–37; 15:11–32.

flourish with a soft heart in the rough and tumble of the marketplace? Yes. And the fact you have a heart to do that indicates you are thriving in the kingdom of God.

Sign Six: *Being Single-Minded.* The term "pure in heart" does not necessarily mean sinlessness, though generations of believers have thought that this was the primary meaning of the phrase. The monastic movement has generally taken this latter view more or less. The Greek word used here, *katharoi,* communicates not sinlessness but being full of integrity, not being double-minded, being unfeigned, or rather being single-eyed (see Matt 6:22). The single-minded are unmixed, unadulterated, unalloyed. The single-eyed are those who see. The double-minded are two-souled and blind. They are duplicitous. They do not see correctly. "Who can stand in his holy place?" asks the psalmist. He answers himself, "The one who has clean hands and a pure heart" (Ps 24:3–4). With this we can see God at work everywhere. And ultimately we know as we are known (Gal 4:9; 1 Cor 13:12; 1 John 3:3). Can you thrive with being single-minded in a marketplace inclined to embrace short-term goals and where black-and-white ethics are often taken over by the color gray? Yes, because all human enterprise is based on trust and you can trust someone who is "pure in heart." That's kingdom thriving.

Sign Seven: *Becoming a Bridge Builder.* "The peacemakers" bring peace—not just quietness, but wholeness and reconciliation—wherever they go. They are not *peace-lovers* doing everything they can to avoid conflict. They are *peacemakers.* They promote soundness, well-being, and wholeness, restoration of harmony between people and with creation. Behind this is the Hebrew word *shalom,* which usually gets translated "peace" but it is a vigorous wall-breaking peace (Eph 2:14–18). As Cornelius Plantinga, quoted earlier, writes: "Shalom, in other words, is the way things ought to be."[15] The shalom-bringers are called sons and daughters of God because they are. Yes, it is costly as you will be attacked by both sides and we must, as my old boss used to say to me, "bear the pain of the organization," the pain of broken relationships and the groaning of the organizational culture. This is why the Beatitudes end with a very negative affirmation, one which in Matthew has an extended explanation (Matt 5:11–12).

Sign Eight: *Embracing Hopeful Perseverance.* "Persecuted for righteousness" means you are facing hardships for doing the right thing and being on the right road. Darrell Johnson calls these people "Happy

---

15. Quoted in Alexander and Brown, eds., *To Whom Shall We Go?*, 35.

Subversives."[16] Why congratulate people for being persecuted? Because it is a sign they are in the kingdom, doing kingdom business, and engaging in kingdom mission. They are in good company. Jesus got into trouble for doing the right thing (and so will his followers). This is the clash of world systems because the kingdom of God is already breaking into this age. Mortimer Arias observes, "The kingdom is reversal and, as such, the permanent subverter of human orders."[17] And behind this is the wonderful truth that we have the kingdom now, not just when we finally get to heaven.

Are These Virtues Practical?

Can you operate this way in the marketplace? Down at the store where you work as a checkout employee? In the president's office high in the tower? On the shop floor if you are machinist? In the home with all the conflicting agendas and ego needs of family life? In a government office?

Martin Luther spoke about left-handed and right-handed power. Speaking to this, Robert Farrar Capon says,

> Unlike the power of the right hand (which, interestingly enough, is governed by the logical, plausibility-loving left hemisphere of the brain), left-handed power is guided by the more intuitive, open and imaginative right side of the brain. Left-handed power, in other words, is precisely paradoxical power: power that looks for all the world like weakness, intervention that seems indistinguishable from non-intervention. . . . It is power—so much power, in fact, that it is the only thing in the world that evil can't touch. God in Christ died forgiving.[18]

On the one hand these virtues do not look very practical. Can you be successful and meek at the same time? If you are merciful will people not take advantage of you? They will. If you are longing for righteousness how will you sell the product that you know has some deficiencies? If you are single-minded, tell the truth, and are not ambivalent, how will you survive in a postmodern workplace where all absolutes are relative? Maybe in the short run people with right-handed power may seem to get ahead and be successful. But in the long run these qualities and left-handed power will win. These virtues work but they work in a different way.

16. Johnson, *Beatitudes*, 128–42.

17. Arias, *Announcing the Reign of God*, 43.

18. Capon, *Parables of the Kingdom*, 19–20.

All business and all human exchange is based on trust. Would you trust someone who does not communicate that she or he is all-sufficient in themselves? Can you trust people who are their own gods? Would you not value to work with someone who makes peace in the workplace? In the workplace is it not a blessing to find mercy, to be given a second chance and to profit from failure and mistakes?

The Seven Beatitudes Rewritten for Business and Not-for-Profit Enterprises

I have recast the Beatitudes for people involved in enterprise such as business or not-for-profits. Here they are:

> I will think much of God and others, and little of myself—poor in spirit
>> I will admit when I am wrong and grieve for sin—mourn
>> I will yield rights for the betterment of others—the meek shall inherit the earth
>> I will desire to do the right thing and to please God in every situation—hunger and thirst for righteousness
>> I will show kindness and grace when others let me down—merciful
>> I will cultivate "a single eye" having all my life focused on God and God's kingdom—pure in heart
>> I will try to bring together factions and people at odds, building community—peacemakers
>> I will "take" the pain of doing the right thing—persecuted because of righteousness.[19]

Practical? You bet they are. For work—it will thrive; for workers—they will flourish; and for the workplace—it will be a taste of heaven and last, possibly, forever. But it is not easy and there are costs involved in being kingdom workers: sometimes monetary costs, vocational costs, emotional costs, and relational costs.

19. These rewritten Beatitudes are found on the "Doing God's Business" film, video #10 available at the IMT website: https://imtglobal.org.

How Do You Get These Virtues?

Virtues are different from values. Values are cherished ways of behaving. As such, values have no opposites: you have your values and I have mine. But virtues have opposites: vices. And virtues are character traits, ingrained in our hearts and lives. You do not get character change by taking a seminar, doing three easy steps, or even by saying "I want to flourish in the kingdom of God." We get character change in the hammer and heat of life, and in the midst of hard situations when we are confronted with a choice, when we discover in ourselves great need, when we cry out to God for help. Jesus called this repentance and said that because the kingdom of God has come near we need to repent (Matt 4:17). Repentance means simply turning from self to God, abandoning making something of ourselves and casting our hearts on Jesus, embracing the kingdom as our most brilliant hope for this life and the next. So, while not actually saying it in the Beatitudes in these actual words, as Servais Pinckaers put it, "All this, in order to prepare a place within us for the seed of new life."

To Whom Shall We Go? is an extraordinary book crafted around the Beatitudes during the pandemic. In this book Irene Alexander and Christopher Brown have crafted prayers on the assumption that, as Segundo Galilea said, the Beatitudes incite us into communion with Christ himself.

Beatitude Prayers

Blessed are the poor in spirit,
for theirs is the kingdom of heaven.

Lord, you always welcome our troubled souls,
and especially when we are at the end of our rope.
Your delight is to form us into the likeness of Jesus,
and though we are poor in spirit,
you refashion us as citizens of your kingdom.
Despite what burdens us,
you call us blessed and open to us your spacious
and generous kingdom realm.

Blessed are those who mourn,
for they will be comforted.

Lord, in the spaciousness and safety of your enfolding,
you encourage us to acknowledge our losses.

These include things we have held dear,
also our shadowy parts—poor attachments and illusions,
which have been unmasked in this time of crisis.
You offer your comfort as we grieve and lament these losses.
And you invite us to a place of receptivity and new life.

Blessed are the meek,
for they will inherit the earth.

Lord, as we let go of, and grieve what we once held dear,
you empower us to grow in the gentle kingdom qualities
of humility and kingdom-heartedness,
where our identity and our vocation is found in you.
As we embrace humility before God, before each other and before nature,
we become your holy sanctuary, here on earth as it is in heaven,
and you invite us to become agents of your kingdom here amid our
troubled world.

Blessed are those who
hunger and thirst for righteousness,
for they will be filled.

Lord, you place within us a renewed passion,
a hunger and thirst for God's reign of righteousness and
justice here on earth,
right in the midst of our upheavals.
You invite us into the self-emptying and sacrificial self-giving
of the Trinity,
and through embracing your way of vulnerability,
we open ourselves to be filled by you.

Blessed are the merciful,
for they will receive mercy.

Lord, we live under your wide and tender mercy
with all aspects of our lives mattering to you.
You enliven within us a spirit of mercy and compassion reflective of your
own, so that those around us matter as they matter to you.
Mercy and compassion are marks of our kingdom character.
You invite us to care deeply and soulfully for others,
to pray for them and be present to them,
knowing that we are eternally enfolded in your loving embrace.

Blessed are the pure in heart, for they will see God.

Lord, you redeem our hearts, reconcile them to you,
and transform them into the likeness of your own transparent heart.
It is through the gift of your indwelling presence

that we are invited to look at ourselves and others,
through your eyes and through the Spirit-illuminated eyes of our hearts.
Lord, help us to discern your presence
amid the crises and upheavals of our day so that we can see
you more clearly,
love you more dearly, and follow you more nearly.

Blessed are the peacemakers,
for they will be called children of God.

Lord, you say to us:
"My peace I leave with you; my peace I give to you.
I do not give to you as the world gives.
Do not let your hearts be troubled, and do not let them be afraid"
(John 14:27 NRSV). It is your peace, not the peace the world gives,
that we so need amid this pandemic crisis. You invite us to take your
peace into our being,
and to become your peacemakers in the interpersonal and group
settings in which you place us,
encouraging cooperation and self-giving rather than competition
and contest.
Offering your way of peace becomes another mark of
our kingdom character.

Blessed are those who are
persecuted for righteousness' sake,
for theirs is the kingdom of heaven.

Lord, you offer us no illusions for our kingdom citizenship.
Rather you animate us with the courage and the mettle we
need to experience persecution for your sake and the sake of
the kingdom (Matt 5:3–10).
Above all,
you offer us hope and your presence in circumstances of
upheaval and crisis,
so that we can walk in the footsteps of your prophets, embody
and reflect your way, and anticipate the fullness of new life
which is to come.[20]

---

20. Alexander and Brown, eds., *To Whom Shall We Go?*, 1, 11, 26, 36, 50, 62, 79, 90.

PART FOUR

Serving the Kingdom in the Marketplace

9

Kingdom Ministry
Transcending Clericalism in the Marketplace

I am recovering the claim that Jesus was not crucified in a cathedral between two candles,
but on a cross between two thieves; on the town garbage heap; on a crossroads so cosmopolitan that they had to write his title in Hebrew and in
Latin and in Greek.

—George McLeod[1]

MINISTRY IN THE MARKETPLACE? It draws up images of intruders pound-
ing at people's hearts with their Bible open and their mouths flaming. Or
more subtly, and more positively, it can be envisioned as a churchgoing
person urging others in the workplace to attend a revival meeting, an in-
home Bible study, or just to attend their church to hear the good news of
Jesus. What is the problem with these two pictures? The problem originates
with the definition of ministry. Unfortunately, most people define ministry
by what they see "the" minister doing—preaching, administering the sacraments, and caring for the spiritual needs of people. This definition creates
a compounded problem for people in Christ who are not declared pastors
or missionaries. If ministry is evangelizing the lost and edifying the found,
then only a small minority of the church can do ministry continuously,
perhaps 1 percent that can be supported financially for "full-time" ministry.

1. MacLeod, *Only One Way Left,* 38.

For the rest of the people of God ministry is a discretionary time activity—something done with the few hours that can be squeezed out of the week's schedule after working, sleeping, householding, neighboring, washing, and doing the chores.[2] Let me develop this wrong definition of ministry because ministry is an "accordion" word has come to mean whatever hot air we put into it!

What is Ministry?

Sometimes ministry is defined by (1) *place* (i.e., work in the church rather than the marketplace and home), (2) *function* (i.e., done on behalf of the whole, such as priestly/pastoral ministration), (3) *need* (i.e., meeting "spiritual" needs rather than secular needs such as preparing a meal for a family), and (4) *title* (i.e., "Reverend"). The Bible, in contrast, addresses this massive confusion with a liberating perspective: ministry is *service to God and on behalf of God in the church and the world.* Ministers are people who put themselves at the disposal of God for the benefit of others and God's world. So, we can do kingdom ministry in the world as well as the church, which is why we have subtitled this chapter "transcending clericalism."

Kingdom ministry, in contrast with the narrow view of ministry rife within the church, is full-time ministry for everyone. There is no part-time option for followers of the King. Further, kingdom ministry is holistic, integral, and incarnational.

The Hebrew words for ministry can mean service as well as ministry. One of the most common Old Testament words for service is *'abad*. *'Abad* combines the meaning of "to work or to make" and in later usage "to worship." The second word, *sharat*, also falls into two categories: personal service rendered to an important personage, such as a ruler (Gen 39:4), and the ministry of worship on the part of those who stand in a special relationship to God, such as priests (Exod 28:35). Then, in the Old Testament, there is the enigmatic *servant of the Lord* in Isaiah 42–53. An hourglass emerges: the national Israel at the top (possibly suggested by Isa 42:19), the spiritual Israel (Isa 41:8–10) in the narrow portion, the Messiah in the neck, as the culmination of the servant-motif (Isa 52:13–53:12), and in Christ (as the hourglass now widens) the service includes the whole people of God, followers of the Servant. As we will see, the Greek word for ministry (*diakonia*) means simply "service." This approach to ministry transcends clericalism.

2. Some of this chapter is extracted from Stevens, *Other Six Days,* 131–90.

Ministry is not an exceptional, optional activity for the people of God, but rather a continuous part of their life. It is service arising from life in the Servant, which takes us into the life of the Father, through the Spirit (as is apparent from Matt 25:42–44). Presbyters, overseers, pastors, and deacons are given as Spirit-gifts for empowering the whole people of God as God's royal priesthood (kingly and priestly) and God's prophetic people (prophets). Church leaders are essential for the right ordering of the community, for drawing out giftedness and nurturing people in the headship of Jesus. Leaders are needed to equip the saints, and to build up the body (Eph 4:11–12). Rather than having the church assist them to do the work of ministry, church leaders are *assistants* to the rest of the body to empower them for their service in church and world. With some delicacy Thomas Gillespie considers what must happen for the reinstatement of the ministry of the whole people of God. "It will be realized only if the 'nonclergy' are willing to move up, if the 'clergy' are willing to move over, and if all of God's people are willing to move out."[3] It is the moving out that marks the kingdom ministry, because kingdom ministry takes place mostly in the world, though not exclusively.

Prophets, Priests, and Kings

In Scripture there are three ministry roles or personages: prophets, who speak the word of God with immediacy and directness; priests, who mediate God's presence to people and build bridges between alienated people; and princes, who function as regents of our God and King in that regents act in leadership on behalf of an absent monarch or when the monarch is not of mature years. But here, again, is a problem. These roles have been attributed to functions exclusively within the church gathered. Yves Congar, the French theologian, did a lot of the advance theological work in preparation for Vatican II, that explosion of ministry that took place among the whole people of God in the Roman Catholic Church. Sadly, he said there will always be laypersons in their place in the church: kneeling before the altar, sitting under the pulpit, and having their hand in the purse.[4] He showed by his biblical research that princes, prophets, and priests were not referring in Scripture to the pope, the bishop, and the parish priest, as had

---

3. Gillespie, "Laity in Biblical Perspective," 327.
4. Congar, *Lay People in the Church*, xi.

largely obtained in the church until Vatican II.[5] He notes how there is a progressive concentration of anointed leadership under the old covenant in Christ and, after Christ, an expansive inclusion of the whole people of God in the prophethood, priesthood, and kingdom rule of all believers. His explosive discovery was that prophets, priests, and princes were the universal dignity of the people of God in Christ, even though he unfoundedly proposed that the New Testament "presupposes the hierarchical priesthood."[6] The Protestant church, while giving lip service to the "priesthood of all believers," a watchword of the Reformation, still largely maintains a hierarchy of ministries with the pastor the minister par excellence.[7]

Let me restate these three biblical roles in a way that would be understandable, acceptable, and dynamic in the workplace. Prophets are agitators. Priests are mediators. And kings are motivators.

Exploring as we will the threefold offices under the old covenant is not only a handy way of understanding the ministry of the whole *laos* (people) in Christ. It is a biblically founded expression of the missional identity of the people of God: prophets speaking God's word, priests mediating God's presence, and kings extending the rule of God into all of God's creation. The combination of these three roles was popularized in the sixteenth century but there is a long biblical history to the threefold offices.

Israel needed all three. The priests ministered to the personal and spiritual needs; the prophet to the public and social needs; and the king to the organizational and political needs. All three pointed beyond themselves toward the eternal purposes of God for Israel. Not surprisingly the full messianic ministry of Christ was explained by the Reformers as the fulfillment of these three ministries. And long before the Reformation, Eusebius of Caesarea argued for Christ as prophet, priest, and king from such passages as Deuteronomy 18:15, Psalm 110:4, and Zechariah 6:13. The reasons are understandable. Israel awaited a prophet (Deut 18:15), a priest (2 Sam 7:12–13; Ps 110:4), and a king (Isa 9:6–7; Ps 2:6; 45:6; 110:1–2), three roles that Christ fulfilled in his own person. These three roles have now, in Christ, been fulfilled in the entire people of God. We need to see how this works out in the world, as well as the church. These three roles can

---

5. Congar makes these threefold office the grammar of his theology of the laity, though he comes short of expressing these offices as whole-people ministries. Congar, *Lay People in the Church*, 121–323.

6 Congar, *Lay People in the Church*, 61–62. Congar cites in support Thomas Aquinas, *Summa theologia*, III, q.22.a.1, ad 3, and II-II, q.183, a.2.

7. I refer the reader to my major work on this subject, *Other Six Days*.

be undertaken whether you are a CEO or an entry-level employee, whether you are a volunteer working in your home with a family or a paid government agent.

Agitators: The Prophetic People

Agitators use words to challenge preconceived ideas, assumptions, and the status quo. They are needed in the workplace, needed desperately. Otherwise people would keep on doing the same thing forever or at least until the institution or company grinds to a halt. Agitators speak God's perspective with directness and immediacy and, as you can expect, they are not always liked for doing so.

In the Bible the prophethood of all believers started with the *crie de coeur* of Moses. Moses said, "Are you jealous for my sake? I wish that all the Lord's people were prophets and that the Lord would put his Spirit on them!" (Num 11:25–29). Joel had a more complete vision for the last days: "And afterward, I [God] will pour out my Spirit on all people. Your sons and your daughters will prophesy, your old men will dream dreams, your young men will see visions. Even on my servants, both men and women, I will pour out my Spirit in those days" (Joel 2:28). So on the day of Pentecost, Peter, quoting these words, significantly changed "and afterward" (Joel 2:28) into "in the last days," since the whole of Joel's prophecy was about the "end time" (Acts 2:17–18). The last days of fulfillment had arrived with the outpouring of the eschatological (end-time) Spirit. Then through the outpouring of the Spirit on the whole people of God all believers were equipped to prophesy, not just a few special anointed messengers like Moses, Isaiah, and Hosea. Along with the "priesthood of all believers" popularized in the Reformation, we could coin another phrase.

The Prophethood of All Believers

The church is God's greatest prophet/preacher in history. All kingdom people are spokespersons for the gospel of the kingdom through "verbal signing." This is the burden of Jesus' teaching[8] and the preoccupation of early Christians.[9] And the first duty of the preacher-pastor in the church

---

8. See Mark 1:14–15; Luke 4:21; 4:43; Matt 10:7; 24:14.
9. See, for example, Acts 8:12; 14:22; 19:8; 28:23, 31.

is to equip the whole church to preach, not necessarily in the formal sense of sermonizing but in the informal meaning of using words to declare the good news of the kingdom of God having come near.[10] This is part of building up the body of Christ so that believers will no longer be "infants" (Eph 4:11–14). Leaders do this by equipping all the people of God to be able to open God's word and to hear God speak *for themselves*. Who could have designed a system, as has surely happened, by which people can hear a sermon each Sunday for the whole of their lives and not be able to open the Bible for themselves? Speaking to the inversion of the biblical vision, the radical missiologist Roland Allen said, "It would be better to teach a few [people] to call on the name of the Lord for themselves than to fill the church with people who have given up idolatry, slavishly and unintelligently, and have acquired the habit of thinking that it is the duty of converts to sit and be taught and to hear prayers read for them in the church by a paid mission agent."[11]

What does this mean for the ministry of the people of God under the new covenant? First, every believer is called and equipped by God to bear witness to the gospel of the kingdom of God and to bring God's word to the world. Second, the prophethood of all believers means that each Christian should be ready to bring God's word "in season" (when prepared and expected) and "out of season" (when the opportunity comes unexpectedly and inconveniently—2 Tim 4:2). Third, every believer has the heart of God and can speak from the perspective of God's kingdom where things are going, defining reality as well as the vision of the future. But, while every believer has some capacity to prophetic ministry, some believers are gifted especially in this area.

Agitating Ministry in the Marketplace

So how does this work out in the marketplace for the individual believer? John Dalla Costa is a Canadian business consultant who has written a spiritually deep book on work. He answers the question of whether you can be in full-time ministry and do "the Lord's work" in the marketplace (or anywhere else in life) with these descriptive words of functioning as a prophet in the marketplace. Prophets in the workplace

---

10. Forsyth, *Positive Preaching and the Modern Mind*, 53. On equipping the church for word ministry, see Stevens, *Equipper's Guide to Every-Member Ministry*.

11. Allen, *Missionary Methods*, 160–61.

- Agitate
- Criticize
- Inspire
- Dislocate
- Humanize
- Reorient
- Point
- Incite
- Debate
- Proclaim[12]

Prophets, however, need priests and kings. This was true even under the Old Testament. When Hilkiah the high priest found the lost book of the law in the temple, he read the Scripture to King Josiah. The king tore his robes in expression of repentance for the people's neglect of the covenant. He ordered the priest Hilkiah to inquire of the Lord who did so by speaking to Huldah the prophetess (2 Kgs 22:8–14). Then the prophetess declared the outcome of the matter—judgment on the nation and mercy to the king for his spiritual responsiveness. The king then administered the law of God in the nation, implementing the terms of the covenant (23:1–25). This same community of prophet, priest, and king, formed of a few stated individuals under the Old Testament, now is a community of people under the new covenant.

Mediators: The Priestly People

Priests mediate between God and humankind, and between persons and groups that are estranged from each other. The pictorial image for the priest is a bridge builder connecting two sides or two groups of people. This image is drawn from the Latin word for priest, *pontifex*, meaning literally bridge maker, from *pons* bridge plus *fex*, from *facere*, to make. So priests in the workplace build bridges between God and people and between estranged parties. They have the touch of God in doing so. Recently I interviewed a just-retired person from one of the world's largest public

12. Costa, *Magnificence at Work*, 177.

relations companies. He reported that often in his chairmanship people would say things like, "Talking with you makes me feel that I am talking with a priest"—the touch of God. But this person also mediates between factions and builds bridges between people who are not even talking with each other—bridge making.

The biblical basis of the revolutionary doctrine of the priesthood of all believers is one major reference in 1 Peter 2:9: "But you are a chosen people, a royal priesthood, a holy nation, God's special possession," and three minor references in the last book of the Bible, Revelation 1:6, 5:10, and 20:6. But there is more to the priesthood of all believers than a few obscure verses in the New Testament. This intriguing idea gathers up many other New Testament themes, such as universal ministry, universal empowerment in the Spirit, universal calling. It also fulfils the seminal idea planted in the infancy of Israel's story that God's people would be a "kingdom of priests" (Exod 19:6).

The priesthood of all believers was a watchword of the Protestant Reformation. Luther said, "All Christians are priests and all priests are Christians. Anathema to him who distinguishes the priest from the simple Christian."[13] Luther argued that the simple milkmaid or the tailor with the word of God in her or his hands was able to please God and minister the things of God as effectively as the priest, the prelate, and the pope himself. "Ordination does not make a priest, but a servant of priests . . . a servant and an officer of the common priesthood."[14]

The Mediating Community

First, the ministry of the people of God derives from the permanent high priesthood of Jesus; it is not self-generated. Because of this every believer has direct access to God through Jesus and does not need the penances and absolution of a human priest, Jesus is enough. Because Jesus ever lives to intercede on our behalf, and because believers are joined to the Lord, the believing community is a priestly community in which every believer might well be called a priest. Second, all believers participate in the continuing priestly ministry of Christ; it is not now undertaken representatively or vicariously by a select few. Luther discovered what we now know to be the unequivocal truth, that the argument for a special or a clerical

13. Quoted in Fischer, "Luther on the Priesthood of All Believers," 298.
14. Quoted in Fischer, "Luther on the Priesthood of All Believers," 303.

priesthood must be made on some other grounds than the New Testament. This priesthood is corporate as well as individual. Finally, the priesthood of believers is both *ecclesial* (in the gathered life of the church) and *diasporic* (in the dispersed life of the church). To show the missionary implications of the priesthood of Jesus, the author of Hebrews says in 13:13, "Let us, then, go to him outside the camp, bearing the disgrace he bore."

What Mediators Do in the Workplace

Mediators bring the touch of God to people and places. They touch God on behalf of people and places through prayer and intercession. Adam and Eve were priests bringing the presence and glory of God to the earth that they were called to fill. They also lifted up, before they sinned, the whole of their life in thanksgiving and praise to God, as what Paul in Romans 12:1–2 speaks of as a "spiritual worship."

There is priestly ministry through service in the world. There are obvious ways we may do this, such as helping the helpless. There are strategic ways, such as asking why the poor are poor and dealing with the structures and powers of our societies that marginalize and depersonalize people; thus we become priests to the principalities and powers (Eph 3:10). There are also earthy ways in which priestly ministry can touch people and places for God in homes, workplaces, neighborhoods, and whole societies. The priesthood of Adam and Eve in the garden was an embodied ministry— naming, cultivating, integrating, releasing potential, envisioning, creating, offering what Robert Farrar Capon calls "the oblation of things."[15] This priestly ministry takes place in homes, school rooms, offices and factories, on planes and buses, in government offices and artist studios, as well as in churches.

Imagine a worker on a hobbing machine in a precision gear manufacturing company. She is not the CEO or even the foreperson. But she knows that she is a priest-mediator and she prays for the other workers within her circle of influence. She dedicates her work to God with prayer and thanksgiving. She does the work and labors "in the Lord." At coffee breaks and lunch hours she talks with co-workers, bearing their lives up to God (silently) in prayer. She mentors them, helping them with their relational struggles, their priorities, and even their work ethic. She is a marketplace pastor. From time to time, workers sense that she is a caring, sensitive, and

---

15. Capon, *An Offering of Uncles*, 163.

spiritual person and they confide in her. And from time to time, she is able to put in a good word for Jesus and the coming kingdom. And sometimes someone responds to her question, "Would you like me to pray for you?" with a "Yes." That is marketplace ministry.

Costa says that priests in the workplace do some of the following things:

- Consecrate

- Empathize

- Enable

- Educate

- Divinize

- Reveal

- Anoint

- Reflect

- Discourse

- Pray[16]

Now we must turn to the intriguing and usually neglected first half of the phrase "*royal* priesthood" in 1 Peter 2:9. It is seldom noticed that in all but the final reference to the priesthood of believers in Revelation 20:6 the priesthood is linked with kingship or sovereign rule. The reinstatement of the royal dimension of the ministry of the people of God is critical for the ministry of the whole people of God especially in the world. It is part of kingdom ministry.

Motivators: The Kingly People

A key question in managing others is whether the motivational switch is inside a person or outside. That is, can managers function in ways that actually motivate people or is the motivational switch so deeply embedded in the person's psyche that there is nothing managers can do other than to command people to do their duty? I have pondered this question deeply and have concluded that it is both-and, both inside and outside. And really great managers, whether of a team or a whole community, try to channel

16. Costa, *Magnificence at Work*, 177.

the innate motivation of their members in the direction of the goal of the organization, the business, or the enterprise. This is especially true in the kingdom of God, which is the greatest enterprise of all and the one that encompasses all we hope and dream about for humankind on earth.

I, for example, am an entrepreneur. I love starting things, bringing a creative edge to an existing project. I have in my lifetime started organizations, planted churches, developed educational programs, started businesses, and most recently started the Institute for Marketplace Transformation. But an entrepreneur must be able to invent *and* manage. The patent office is full of inventions that have never seen the light of day. Why? Because invention or innovation is not enough. So to manage me, and that is no easy task, a leader has to know me and direct my creativity towards the goal of the organization, which is what good leaders do. But good leaders are motivators in a second sense by defining reality, giving vision, and saying thanks, as leadership guru Max DePree was fond of saying.[17]

Motivators in the Marketplace

These royal rulers exercise dominion *personally* as they walk in the Spirit and triumph over the flesh—the self turned inward and away from God (Rom 7:1–25; Gal 5:16–26). Christians govern their passions, exercise self-control, put their lives in order, and live as royal creatures. They are also royal rulers *ecclesiastically*—in the church. They share Christ's rule as Head and King. Paul's ironic outburst to the Corinthians suggests that by putting the church in order relationally, socially and morally they should have been functioning as royalty: "You have begun to reign—and that without us! How I wish that you really had begun to reign so that we also might reign with you!" (1 Cor 4:8). They also share in the rule of the world *cosmically* in a prophetic, preliminary, and anticipatory way as they live now in the kingdom but wait, work, and pray for the full coming of the kingdom: now but not yet. As kings and queens in the world, men and women are called to exercise dominion *vocationally in the world* (Gen 1:26, 28), a distinctively royal role,[18] though in this partially redeemed world "man is a toilful and anxious king, who has to subdue his realm inch by inch, with unceasing labour."[19]

17. See De Pree, *Leadership Is an Art*, 9.
18. Dumbrell, *End of the Beginning*, 42.
19. Congar, *Lay People in the Church*, 237.

Again John Dalla Costa notes that princes and princesses, regents, kings and queens in the workplace do some or all of the following:

- Integrate
- Symbolize
- Empower
- Adjudicate
- Systemize
- Restructure
- Appoint
- Wisen
- Dialogue
- Pronounce[20]

Agitators, Mediators, and Motivators in the Marketplace

Taken together the threefold office expresses every member ministry in the marketplace as well as the church. Taken together they constitute kingdom ministry in the marketplace.

Years ago, George MacLeod of the Iona Community wrote about mission in the marketplace in these closing words.

> I simply argue that the cross be raised again at the centre of the market place as well as on the steeple of the church . . . ; at the kind of place where cynics talk smut, and thieves curse, and soldiers gamble. Because that is where he died and that is what he died about. And that is where churchmen should be and what churchmen should be about.[21]

20. Costa, *Magnificence at Work*, 177.
21. Quoted in Harkness, *Church and Its Laity*, 156.

10

Kingdom Mission
Transcending Mission through Business

"The marketplace is the last mission frontier."

—Ed Silvoso[1]

"Mission means the announcements of Christ's lordship over all reality and an invitation to submit to it."

—David Bosch[2]

SO WHAT DOES MISSION in and through the marketplace look like? Is it planting a business, sometimes called a "fake" business, in a restricted access country solely in order to evangelize? Is it simply making as much money as you can in order to financially support "the Lord's work"? Is it having lunchtime Bible studies or placing a tract in each product sold in your store? Is it direct evangelism in the workplace, inviting people to consider the Four Spiritual Laws or the Three Biblical Principles? Perhaps, if you are allowed to do it! But especially in a post-Christendom, postmodern, post-Christian Western context these might not even be possible. In Africa, where my wife and I have spent several years, all of these direct mission interventions are more than possible. They are welcome, especially in rural

1. Quoted in Johnson, "Toward a Marketplace Missiology," 87.
2. Bosch, *Transforming Mission*, 148.

113

Africa. But not where I live now. These "marketplace mission" initiatives, maybe what I am calling "mission through business," are part of but not the whole of kingdom mission.

Typically we think of business through mission as a way to reach a "closed country" (closed, that is, to professional missionaries), but where people are, nevertheless, "open" to the good news—possibly "easy to reach." But in this chapter we will be exploring the role of business and other forms of human enterprise in countries and cultures that are technically "open" to pastors and missionaries, but are "hard to reach" because they have been inoculated against the faith by mild doses of the real thing. This includes countries like Canada. Tetsunao Yamamori, in his *On Kingdom Business: Transforming Missions Through Entrepreneurial Strategies*, notes how, in the cross-cultural world, Muslims, Hindus, and Buddhists have been largely

> impervious to our evangelism. . . . To reach such people, we need to not only tell them about the gospel but also to *show* it to them. How do we do this in the context of today's globalizing economy, in which people's felt needs center more on finding a job and at-taining economic development than on investigating the claims of Christ? In a word, the answer is "business," or, to be more precise, "kingdom business."[3]

Earlier I noted that the West, not universally of course but mostly, is in the "hard to reach" category because of postmodern, post-Christian, and post-church thinking—really *anti*-Christian thinking and culture. There are exceptions of course, but it calls for a different strategy. And that strat-egy is marketplace mission—mission that is subversive of the dominant culture. If you, the reader, happen to live and work in a country or culture that welcomes the Christian way, thank God, but be ready for a change because, I suspect, it is coming. But first we must explore the relationship of business and mission.

---

3. Yamamori and Eldred, eds., *On Kingdom Business*, 7, emphasis his. In Appendix D of this book, filled with case studies, Steve Rundle and Patrick Lai list works from *Mar-ketplace Annotated Bibliography* by Pete Hammond, R. Paul Stevens, and Todd Svanoe that apply to this mission focus, 325–37.

The Awkward Marriage of Business and Mission

Dwight Baker in a journal article entitled "Mission Geometry" plots the coordinates of Business as Mission.[4]

- Business **opposed** to mission—outright opposition in the name of business profits

- Business **subverting** mission—business drawing missionaries away from their missional commitments

- Business **capitalizing** on mission—how missionaries have been forerunners and pathbreakers for commerce

- Business **relying on** mission—employment of nationals by missionaries becoming clerks and functionaries in commercial enterprises

- Business **enabling** mission—business providing infrastructure in roads, communication, and support services for mission

- Business **inherent in** mission—mission agencies having systems of management and governance for acquiring personnel and resources

- Business **funding** mission—Protestant missions being funded by companies developed for that express purpose

- Business **dictating** mission—philanthropists and wealthy people using money to determine what mission is actually done

- Business **auxiliary** to mission—William Carey started a printing plant to publish Bibles and tracts

- Business **ancillary** to mission—businesses that, while not directly related to mission, are serviceable instruments for mission

- Business **as** mission—"this segment of Great Commission companies is intended to provide entry into otherwise 'closed' or restricted countries and supplies reasons for their government to tolerate Christian witness."[5] (I will come back to this definition as I am unhappy with it.)

Baker then looks at the marriage from the perspective of mission:

- Mission **opponent of** businesses—David Livingstone spoke out against land grabs in South Africa and the slave trade

---

4. Baker, "Missional Geometry."
5. Baker, "Missional Geometry," 47.

- Mission **buffer against** businesses—many missionaries have acted as change agents to prepare the people to deal with traders and the people who would dominate them

- Mission **generator of** businesses—missionaries are often living advertisements for Western goods

- Mission as **ally of** business—mission has enlarged the pool of employees for Western enterprises

- Mission as **template for** business—mission agencies in situations where the infrastructure is broken can model flexible and efficient organizations

- Mission as **exemplar for** business—for example, "every African knows that it is to missionaries that they owe the beginning of the African educational system."[6]

- Mission **indebted to** businesses—merchants underwrote the ventures in mission

- Mission **supplicating** businesses—mission agencies looking to the business world for models and for resources

- Mission **founding auxiliary** businesses—mission agencies creating hospitals, radio stations, and orphanages for mission purposes

- Mission **founding ancillary** businesses—mission agencies establishing businesses to generate funds for mission, sometimes called "tentmakers." "[T]entmakers became job *takers*, at best displacing national workers . . . rather than job *makers*, creating new jobs for local residents."[7]

- Mission via **strategic** business—"Business as mission, in my understanding of current discussion, consists of entrepreneurial activity conceived of and carried out in such a way that a single entity fulfils a dual role. One role is financial and economic. . . .The other role is spiritual and missional, leading to salvation, spiritual growth and facilitation of fellowships of followers of Jesus Christ *in otherwise politically closed or restricted settings,*" says Baker.[8]

---

6. Baker, "Missional Geometry," 51.
7. Baker, "Missional Geometry," 53, emphasis mine.
8. Baker, "Missional Geometry," 54, emphasis mine.

This last quotation is, in my view, too restrictive since business as mission need not be in a restricted access country. But to say the least it is an odd marriage. Some would say they are an incompatible couple. The one, business, is there for profit through the provision of goods or services. The other, mission, is for new life, freely given, through announcing and embodying the reign of God. Has God put these two together, and "what God has joined together, let no one separate" (Matt 19:6)—or are they essentially unsuited partners? Sadly, some would say it is better to relegate business (and other marketplace enterprises) to the realm of the secular and keep mission in the arena of the sacred. To answer this question of the seemingly awkward relationship of business and mission we must explore the question of what is the mission of God.[9]

God's mission begins with creation and is embodied in the teaching and work of Jesus. All of humankind is invited into the mission of the triune God in what I have called "the *greatest* commission": "As the Father has sent me [literally, missioned me with all the resources of the triune God], I am sending you [in a fully incarnational mission]" (John 20:21). It is more than the usual interpretation of the so-called "Great Commission" in Matthew 28:18–20.[10]

As Bosch says, noted above, "Mission means the announcement of Christ's lordship over all reality and an invitation to submit to it." This involves: *proclamation* (it is here), *annunciation* (it is coming), *denunciation* (declaring what is unjust and opposed to the rule of God), *embodiment* (in the community of the King), *compassion and consolation* (to those sinned against), *continuing conversion* (like Peter's continuing conversion), and *confronting the powers*.[11] This includes creational stewardship, economic justice, community building, restored relationship with God, and restored community and neighboring. Chris Wright, a mission theologian, says that integral mission involves 1) evangelism, 2) teaching, 3) compassion, 4)

9. Some of this chapter is excerpted from Stevens, *Doing God's Business*, 78–100.

10. I acknowledge my indebtedness to an article by John Jefferson Davis, who traced the history of the interpretation of Matthew 28:18–20 from the early church to the present, showing how the full meaning of the text was obscured by ecclesiastical controversies with the full missiological implication emerging with William Carey. Davis notes that "the marketplace implications of this crucial text are just beginning to receive attention at the present time" (1). See Davis, "'Teaching Them to Observe All that I Have Commanded You.'"

11. Bosch, *Transforming Mission*, 148.

justice, and 5) creation care.[12] In business some of these five call for social responsibility, what is sometimes called the "double bottom line" and sometimes the "triple bottom line"—profit, people, and the planet.[13] So how does business relate to the mission of God?

Unpacking Business as Mission

The reason why we must ask that question is the vast range of definitions and practices given to the contemporary buzzword "business as mission" (BAM). As noted above, the definitions range from starting a fake business in a restricted-access country for the purposes of evangelism, to a fully integrated business and mission in which every part of the business is for the glory of God and the advancing of the kingdom. The massive volume on this subject was written by Neal Johnson, in which he provides his own definition of BAM as follows: "BAM is broadly defined as a for-profit commercial business venture that is Christian led, intentionally devoted to being used as an instrument of God's mission (*missio Dei*) to the world, and is *operated in a cross-cultural environment*, either domestic or international."[14]

Fortunately Johnson includes a definition from Mats Tunehag from the 2004 Lausanne conference that does not restrict BAM to a "cross-cultural environment."

> Business as Mission is about real, viable, sustainable and profitable businesses; with a Kingdom of God purpose, perspective and impact; leading to transformation of people and societies spiritually, economically, socially and environmentally—to the glory of God.[15]

Johnson also wrote an article on "Toward a Marketplace Missiology," for the journal *Missiology*. In this article he affirms that the marketplace is the last and possibly the most neglected mission field. He is not alone in making that claim.

William Carey, sometimes regarded as the founder of modern missions, envisioned the gospel going into all the world through the means of international trade. He drew on the text in Isaiah 60:9: "Surely the islands

---

12. Wright, "Integral Mission and the Great Commission."

13. Alter, *Managing the Double Bottom Line.*

14. Johnson, *Business as Mission,* 27–28, emphasis mine.

15. Quoted in Johnson, *Business as Mission,* 28–29.

look to me; in the lead are the ships of Tarshish, bringing your children from afar, with their silver and gold, to the honour of the Lord your God, the Holy One of Israel, for he has endowed you [Zion] with splendor."[16] In Carey's view it was inexcusable not to go into all the world to preach the gospel now that we have the mariner's compass and can safely cross any sea and indeed do so for trade.[17] International trade, whether on a small scale of entrepreneurial import-export business or the grand scale of a multinational corporation, represents an unprecedented opportunity for believers to be present in the world God loves, to make contacts with people, to earn the right to speak, and to share the wonderful good news of Jesus. It is being done today by thousands of believers in places where the formal missionary is excluded.

Even in so-called "open countries" such as post-Christian Europe and Canada—truly "hard to reach" though not "closed countries"—trade brings us into contact with people who would never darken the door of a church. Commenting on the global picture, Ralph McCall, a venture capitalist residing in Switzerland, proposed that today "the unreached world" is Europe and "the lost tribe" is the multinational corporation.[18]

But let me summarize what I judge is not to be and what should be considered as "business as mission."

First, what is not to be considered as business as mission. Business as mission is *not* business solely to be a platform for evangelism in a restricted-access county. In this case the mission "field" is outside the business and the business people are missionaries. Some have called this a "fake" business, or a "job-taker business." And what happens when people become Christians through this fake business? Having no other models they choose to become pastors or stated missionaries, if they can.

Second, it is questionable whether a business that sets out to meet social needs as a social enterprise is fully a business as mission, even if it is a sustainable enterprise, though often it is a "job taker." Why? The mission field is, once again, outside the business and there is no interest in seeing the business itself as part of God's mission.

---

16. Carey, *An Enquiry*, 68. Carey says, "This seems to imply that in the time of the glorious increase of the church, in the latter days, commerce shall subserve the spread of the gospel."

17. Carey, *An Enquiry*, 67.

18. Heard while McCall was lecturing at Regent College in spring of 1988.

Third, and here is where I come down on the issue, business as mission is a kingdom business that embraces kingdom values and kingdom mission of bringing human flourishing and new life both internally, among stakeholders, and in the society in which it operates. The business itself is part of God's mission, not just existing for "the mission field." *It is both mission field and mission*, and frequently is a job maker. This distinction between mission field and mission is worth making.

Business as Mission Field

The reasons for thinking that the marketplace is a key mission field are so obvious that one could only think that an enemy has blinded our eyes to the possibilities. *First, there is access.* The marketplace gives access to people who work there while it denies access to outsiders, especially religious professionals, except in a few cases where industrial or corporate chaplaincy is accepted. *Second, for most people the workplace is a relational context.* The corporation is a community—literally a company is "*com*"–"*pani*" (shared bread)—a community of shared life and enterprise, providing a relational context for ministry often deeper than the local church or the neighborhood.

Third, there is the matter of sheer time. Most working adults spend most of their waking hours in this community. *Fourth, the marketplace itself raises issues that are openings for the gospel and pastoral care*: identity, relationality, priorities, credibility, life purpose, work-life balance, success and failure. *Fifth, our life is an open book in the workplace.* The opportunities abound for relational evangelism in which a person may hear the gospel not only by word but in the lived out behavior of the witness, especially their way of working. *Sixth, the workplace brings us into proximity to people in need and crisis.* When trouble and hardship hit, a worker is more inclined to share this with a colleague at work than a religious professional in the church.

Consider the transformation that would come if every local church recognized and prayed for not only ordinary members working in businesses but also travelling businesspeople going to other countries with significant opportunities with governments and industries. Are they not as deserving of prayer support and commissioning as a team of people going to a developing country to help build a church building or a home?

Undoubtedly the traditional full-support missionary at home and abroad is up for grabs in many parts of the world. But in the twenty-first century, according to Billy Graham, "one of the next great moves of God is going to be through the believers in the workplace."[19] Accordingly, summarizing the place of marketplace in the mission of God, Neal Johnson says we must approach the marketplace "as a mission field in its own right. . . . It is a place that has a distinctive culture, a unique worldview, and a remarkable capacity to touch virtually every person on earth."[20] To this end Johnson outlines the three ways the marketplace can be a mission field.

The first is "mission *into* the marketplace by outsiders, those who are not participants in the business community, who seek to convert and disciple nonbelievers within the community."[21] The marketplace chaplaincy program does this in part, as well as many organizations that sponsor (usually relying on outsiders to the marketplace and at least one person inside) noon-hour Bible studies. The second track "is mission *within* the marketplace, in which Christians who are participants in the marketplace, and thus insiders, seek to evangelize and disciple, and to network and encourage one another within their own work environment."[22] The third track of marketplace missiology, according to Johnson, is mission *through* the marketplace, where "insiders reach outside the marketplace, utilizing their enormous, God-given influence, resources, and expertise for Christ."[23] My mind goes to a friend who has several car dealerships and uses his influence to do strategic good in his city, including housing, social justice, and education for the marginalized.

But is there more to the kingdom of God than regarding the workplace as a mission field?

Business as Mission

Some years ago I visited the president of a large chain of retail stores in Korea. Initially, he said, he had gone into business to make a lot of money, which he intended to give to missions. He did this. This is mission *through* business. Then he began to see the business was a means of channeling

19. Quoted in Eldred, *God Is at Work*, 46.
20. Johnson, "Toward a Marketplace Missiology," 90.
21. Johnson, "Toward a Marketplace Missiology," 91.
22. Johnson, "Toward a Marketplace Missiology," 91.
23. Johnson, "Toward a Marketplace Missiology," 91.

mission throughout the world. He also did this. Again, mission through business. In Korea these are sometimes called "businaries." Further, he started hiring nonbelievers with a view to leading them to Christ and providing chaplaincy services. But finally he began to understand that the very work he was doing was part of what God wanted done on earth through his mission, though not perfectly of course.

Let me illustrate this by referring to the Medieval Christian theologian Thomas Aquinas. He brilliantly expounded the virtuous life, indeed the missional life, using two tables, the one for corporal almsdeeds (good physical works) and the other for spiritual almsdeeds (good spiritual works).

First let us consider Aquinas's corporal almsdeeds: What do you think of when you hear these?

- To feed the hungry
- To give drink to the thirsty
- To clothe the naked
- To harbor the harborless
- To visit the sick
- To ransom the captive
- To bury the dead

Do you think of the following?

- To feed the hungry (food industry)
- To give drink to the thirsty (beverage)
- To clothe the naked (clothing, design)
- To harbor the harborless (hospitality)
- To visit the sick (medicine, counseling)
- To ransom the captive (police, military)
- To bury the dead (funeral business)

Then let's consider Aquinas's spiritual almsdeeds.

- To instruct the ignorant
- To counsel the doubtful
- To comfort the sorrowful

- To reprove the sinner
- To forgive injuries
- To bear with those who trouble and annoy us
- To pray for all[24]

In these two panels we nicely sum up what we have defined as kingdom mission from Isaiah 61 and the words and deeds of Jesus in Luke 4, namely, good news to the poor, release to the captives, recovery of sight to the blind, announcing the favor of God, universal ministry, and our work. *So the actual work we do in the marketplace—mostly in Aquinas's corporal almsdeeds—is part of, but not all of, the kingdom mission of God. All our work in the messy middle of the grand story (the overlapping of the new age with the old age) are a mixture of good and not so good, kingdom and non-kingdom. But if done for God with faith, hope, and love, they will last and count for the kingdom of God. And the spiritual almsdeeds named by Aquinas can also be done in the marketplace, thus completing the mission of God.*

I suggest with the following the ten characteristics of a kingdom business.

1. The presence of a Christian or Christians with a sphere of influence, whether large or small.

2. A product or service in harmony with God's creational purpose.

3. A mission or business purpose that is larger and deeper than mere financial profit, though including it, so that the business contributes in some way to the kingdom of God.

4. The business or enterprise suggests the presence of the kingdom and invites the opportunity to witness.

5. The customer is treated with dignity and respect and not merely as a means of profit.

6. Employees and workers are equipped to achieve greater potential in their life. If they are Christians they can work wholeheartedly (Col 3:22–25) with faith, hope, and love (1 Cor 13:13; 1 Thess 1:2–3).

7. All aspects of the business are considered to be potentially a ministry and a subject of prayer.

24. Thomas Aquinas, "Treatise on Faith, Hope and Charity," *Summa Theologica*, Part II of second part, Q 32, art 2.

8. The culture of the organization—symbols, values, and governing beliefs—line up essentially with God's word and kingdom purposes.

9. The leaders are servants, dedicated to serve the mission of the business, the best interests of employees, customers, and shareholders
   because they are first of all servants of God.

10. The business runs on grace.[25]

So how in practice can we do this?

Mission in and through the Workplace

First, there is verbal witness. We are called to bear God's word and the good
news of the kingdom in the marketplace as well as everywhere else. To do
this we have to earn the right to speak by our lives and work. Saint Fran-
cis of Assisi is often (if erroneously) attributed with saying, "Preach the
gospel at all times and if necessary use words." But to be ready to give a
reason for the hope within us is a crucial preparedness. While working as
a carpenter I was several weeks on a particular job when the plasterer with
whom I worked asked me at the coffee break, "Paul, what happens when we
die?" This and a dozen other questions invite a kingdom answer. In fact my
co-worker would never ask this of a pastor because he would not darken
the door of a church. To witness to the kingdom of God in Jesus, as Amy
Sherman in *Kingdom Calling* notes, our language needs to change. "Typically congregants are trained to encourage seekers to 'ask Jesus into their
heart.' However, this does not mirror the language Jesus himself used. His
evangelistic invitation was, 'Come, enter my kingdom.'"[26]

Second, there is practical service. We are serving God and God's purposes (the real meaning of "ministry") in the marketplace as we release talents, create community, and serve our neighbor through providing goods
and services. Good work enhances human life, does not use people as mere
instruments, and develops the potential of creation. A village church in
Yorkshire, UK recently honored one of its earlier members with a $90,000
stained glass window. The parishioner was Thomas Crapper, a plumber
born in the nearby village of Thorne in 1836. As reported in the Canadian
paper *The Globe and Mail*, "the window incorporates a tastefully rendered

25. For a more complete exposition of this and how the great commandment might
look when applied to a company, please request an article from registrar@imtglobal.org.

26. Sherman, *Kingdom Calling*, 84.

silhouette of a toilet as part of a celebration of local achievements." Mr. Crapper was the inventor of the flush toilet.[27]

Third, we advance God's kingdom mission by building community in the workplace and globally. We build community by caring for our neighbor in the workplace and creating corporate and professional cultures that reflect in some measure the presence of the kingdom: people-affirming, interdependent communities that give people significance, that release talents and help people learn to love. Even if we are not in senior leadership we have an influence around our workstations and can pray for and build teamwork relationships with our colleagues.

Fourth, we can have a redemptive role in the marketplace. Commenting on the Hebrew word *avodah,* which expresses the three notions of worship, work, and service, Rabbi Michael Strassfeld says, "Work . . . is a form of service to the world, to the rest of humanity, and to God. . . . It has the potential to accomplish *tikkun olam,* 'Repair of the world.'"[28]

Fifth, we may have a prophetic role in the marketplace. We serve God by calling the marketplace to accountability for injustice, rapacious competition, for idolatrous demands made on workers, for unjust and unfair remuneration patterns, and for participation in global inequities. In this way we engage not only individual sin but systemic evil, what Paul called "the principalities and powers." We also work prophetically by pointing to the final consummation of history and the new heaven and new earth, giving meaning to this-worldly activity.

So it is not an either-or, either mission field or mission, but a both-and. Regarding the marketplace as "mission field" serves to build the *faith community* (one of the two dimensions of God's mission); viewing the marketplace as "mission" serves to build the *human community.* Sin pollutes this activity just as much as it twists the direct evangelistic efforts Christians undertake in the world. But taken together, as both mission field and mission, business activity is one way of serving God and God's purposes in the world. We cannot pray "thy kingdom come, thy will be done on earth" without including the possibility that we are both cooperating with God now in accomplishing his will on earth, and praying and working toward the second coming of Christ when the "not yet" and "coming" of the kingdom will become fully "now" and "here."

27. Kroeker, "Dangerous to the Status Quo," 2.
28. Quoted in Sherman, *Kingdom Calling,* 130.

11

Kingdom Leadership
Transcending Mere Pragmatics

"My employees, my customers, and my suppliers are my congregation. My business is my altar."

—A Marketplace Pastor

"Keep watch over yourselves and all the flock of which the Holy Spirit has made you overseers."

—Paul, Acts 20:28

Final goodbyes are significant but hard to give and receive. I remember a stunning farewell I received from church elders in the western fringe of Kenya after a three-day seminar. The lead elder said, "We forgive you for all the mistakes you have made while you were with us!" I was horrified! What had I done? But then he said, "And we trust that you will forgive *us* for our sins against you." On reflection it was beautiful to leave with a clear conscience. I would never, like Paul speaking to the Ephesians, be able to see them again. But these farewell words are not easy to give and even harder to receive. The Apostle Paul was saying goodbye to the elders of the church in Ephesus. He was on his way to Jerusalem and knew that hard times were ahead. This was his last visit. So this departing word was important. "Keep watch over yourselves"—attend to your own spirituality and authenticity—"and [keep watch over] all the flock of which the Holy Spirit has made you overseers"—what leading others actually means (Acts 20:28). We must start with ourselves.

Keeping Watch over Ourselves: Kingdom Leadership Is Authentic

Leadership is influence expressed in relationships, organizations, and communities through which followership is gained and goals are accomplished. The people influenced can number two or two thousand. But there is more. *Spiritual leadership* is influence that arises from the spiritual life of the leader. This means that leadership is more than mere pragmatics—who does what, when, and where. Further spiritual leadership nurtures the spiritual life of the people you are serving. But *kingdom leadership*, incorporating both general leadership and spiritual leadership, has as its purpose the values and goals of the kingdom of God. The values include, as we have seen, integrating, meaning, and thriving, as well as the virtues of the Beatitudes. Salty kingdom values include *forgiveness* and *accountability*—giving people a second chance, going the second mile (Matt 18:21–35; 5:41); *integrity in word and deed*—letting your yes be yes, inner and outer life in synch, transparency (Matt 5:37); *fairness* and *justice*—doing the right thing in compensation, purity of product, handling of money; *extraordinary service*—going beyond duty (Col 4:1; Luke 17:7–10); *boundary-breaking behavior* (Luke 5:27–31); *stewardship*—treasuring the gifts of others, caring for creation, developing a motivating and affirming organizational culture (Matt 25:14–30); *empowerment*—releasing other people's gifts and talents, helping others to thrive in service (Eph 4:11–12); *shalom* and *being socially responsible*—neighbor love personally and socially (Matt 22:39); *joy*—experiencing a God-infusion of exuberance and well-being that is not dependent on circumstances—some have called this "fun" in the workplace (Phil 4:4). So Canon Stanley Evans once described the Christian as a "controlled drunk purposively intoxicated with the joy of the life which is perpetually created by God himself."[1] The goal of kingdom leadership is to lead the organization and its people to harmonize their work and innovation with the present and coming kingdom of God. But the big question is how we gain followers and how to be followers.

---

1. Quoted in Leech, *Experiencing God*, 103.

Gaining Followership

There is an amazing propaganda film about Adolf Hitler produced in 1934 by filmmaker Leni Riefenstahl, called *The Triumph of the Will*.[2] It is said by many today that it is the best propaganda film ever produced, even though it is, as the DVD box says, a "horrifyingly manipulative exercise in propaganda for the Nazi regime." For Riefenstahl it was an art form and she spent the rest of her life dodging the political, social, and ethical implications of her "art form." In the film she portrayed Hitler as a superior person. Speaking to this, Dietrich Bonhoeffer in his little known book *No Rusty Swords* says the Leader—note the capital L—is what no other person can be. This person fuses the individuality of every member of his community into his own persona. The organization led by this person looks healthy but it is really sick. Bonhoeffer speaks to this.

> It is essential for the image of the Leader that the group does not see the face of the one who goes before, but sees him only from behind as the figure stepping out ahead. His humanity is veiled in his Leader's form. . . . The Leader is what no other person can be, an individual, a personality. The relationship between those led and their Leader is that the former transfer their rights to him. It is this one form of the collectivism which turns into intensified individualism. For that reason, the true concept of community, which rests on responsibility, on the recognition that individuals belong responsibly one to another, finds no fulfilment here.[3]

In *The Triumph of the Will* Riefenstahl pictured Hitler coming into Munich in a Mercedes convertible. She positioned her camera at the back of the open vehicle, so you could only see the back of Hitler, not his face, his outstretched arm greeting the crowds who were going crazy. Commenting on this phenomenon, the late Ray Anderson, professor of theology at Fuller Theological Seminary, said,

> True leadership, from a Christian perspective, must be able to preserve a deep sense of community and avoid fusing the needs and desires of the people into a collective unity, with leadership passing over into the role of the Leader. . . . This shift brings a dehumanizing process to those who are being led, and a *veiling of the true humanity of the leader*. . . . He becomes "larger than life,"

2. Riefenstahl, dir., *Triumph of the Will*.
3. Bonhoeffer, *No Rusty Swords*, 186–200.

an object upon which they can project their own individualistic dreams for success and desire for power.[4]

The Character of the Kingdom Leader

In contrast, the apostle Paul as a kingdom leader was vulnerable. His humanity was never veiled. He poured himself out to others just as he was. He said he was knocked down but not knocked out! (2 Cor 11:16–33). He said that when he heard that someone had sinned he burned within (either in indignation or in hateful fascination or both). Indeed, he wrote in 2 Corinthians 3 that we are not like Moses, who had to cover his face when he left the tabernacle communing with the Lord, because the glow was fading! Instead we "with unveiled faces," not role-playing, not appearing larger than life, are actually being transfigured from one degree of glory to another as we look constantly to the Lord. We are like Kodachrome transparencies (when I used to do film photography). If you look *at* the transparency you see almost nothing, except a few wiggles in the emulsion. But if you hold it up to the light and look through it you see a beautiful image.

So **credibility**, essential to gaining followership, is built on authenticity. It is related to transparency, honesty, integrity, and sincerity. **Transparency** is being completely open. Every thought and action is available to others. **Honesty** is telling the truth. **Integrity** is wholeness, soundness. And **sincerity** comes from the Latin *sine ceres*, which means "without wax." Some sculptors in ancient Rome used wax to disguise a chip on a statue. No one would see the flaw until the heat of the sun melted the wax or bad weather eroded it. In this way they were not being perfectly sincere.[5]

Initially at least people tend to trust charisma and credentials, but in the long run they need to trust character. And character is formed in the heat and hammer of life as we respond to God.

But if kingdom leadership involves keeping watch over oneself, it also involves keeping watch over the flock—the people you serve. And this means serving the best interests of followers and caring for the whole person as well as the whole organization. It is more than, but not less than, soul service.

---

4. Anderson, *Minding God's Business*, 79, emphasis mine.

5. Erisman, *Accidental Executive*, 113.

Keeping Watch over the Flock 1: Kingdom Leadership Is Servant Leadership

The kingdom leader is primarily a servant of the Lord. That means that kingdom leadership is essentially spiritual leadership, even if one is leading a business, a political office, or any other human enterprise. Management guru Peter Block defines spirituality in this way: "Spirituality is a process of living out a set of deeply held personal values, of honouring forces or a presence greater than ourselves. It expresses our desire to find meaning in, and to treat as an offering, what we do."[6] That said, in my opinion the best definition of Christian spirituality comes from Segundo Galilea:

> All spirituality springs from this fundamental fact of a God who loved us first. . . . If Christian spirituality is, before all else, an initiative by and a gift from God who loved us and seeks us, spirituality is then our recognition and response, with all that entails, to this love of God that desires to humanize and sanctify us. This path of spirituality is a process, concrete but never finished, by which we identify ourselves with God's plan for creation. Because this plan is essentially the Kingdom of God and its justice (holiness), spirituality is identification with the will of God for bringing this Kingdom to us and others.[7]

On Being a Servant of God

So what does it mean to be a servant of God? A woman comes to our home for two days a week. She serves us. My wife is handicapped so this woman does the laundry, cleans the house, and helps my wife and me. She is a servant. A servant, then, is someone who does what another wishes. And the other whose wishes we want to follow is not primarily the people but the Lord. So a servant of the Lord is a person at the disposal of God to do what God wants. And I think we had better add, "to meet the needs of the world no matter what it costs." There is a reason for the inclusion of "no matter what it costs."

There are four famous passages sometimes called the "servant songs" in the Old Testament book of Isaiah. They are deeply impressive and expressive expressions of "the servant of the Lord." Isaiah 42:1–9 is *the call of*

---

6. Block, *Stewardship*, 48.

7. Galilea, *Way of Living Faith*, 20.

the servant. "Here is my servant, whom I uphold, my chosen one in whom I delight" (42:1) This servant is no demagogue. He does not grab the megaphone on the street (42:2). He has profound respect for the bruised and broken. "A bruised reed he will not break" (42:3). He brings forth justice (42:3–4). Then in Isaiah 49:1–9 the servant experiences frustration. "I have labored in vain. . . . Yet what is due me is in the Lord's hand" (49:4). This is *the vindication of the servant.* But the experience of the servant darkens in the third servant song. Here, in Isaiah 50:4–9, the servant expresses that he has a "well-instructed tongue" (v. 4) from what he has learned in life. But it is not easy. "I offered my back to those who beat me" (v. 6). This is *the Gethsemane of the servant.*

Up until now this enigmatic figure could have been the whole nation of Israel, or perhaps a church within the church, an ideal or spiritual Israel. And finally, as the servant is now focused on one solitary individual in a narrowing like that of an hourglass from the people as a whole—the widest part—to a select few, to now a single individual: the suffering servant in Isaiah 52:13–53:12 of whom it is said that "he bore the sin of many" (53:12), anticipating Jesus the ultimate Servant. This is *the cross of the servant.* Walter Wright, my president at Regent College, used to say to me when I was academic dean, "We have to take the pain of the organization." Others have said something similar.

On Being a Servant of the People

Robert Greenleaf in *Servant Leadership* notes that the servant leader is servant first, not leader first. "The servant-first leader is someone who makes 'sure other people's highest priority needs are being served.'"[8] Where does this service attitude come from?

It does not come as a management technique. Nor is it mere pragmatism. It comes from deep within a person's character, her spirituality, the person whom she serves, indeed from God. After all, when God did not find a servant on earth who could fulfill his service *he became his own servant in the person of Jesus* (Phil 2:7). Jesus put himself at the disposal of the Father to do what the world needed no matter what it would cost. Not surprisingly one of the christological titles of Jesus is the Servant. He is designated such in Acts of the Apostles (3:13; 4:27). So those who follow the Servant must themselves be servants.

8. Greenleaf, *Servant Leadership*, 13.

Accordingly, speaking to service in an organization, Peter Block notes that the servant leader sees that four things obtain:

1. There is a balance of power. People need to act on their own choices.

2. The primary commitment is to the larger community.

3. Each person joins in defining purpose and deciding what kind of culture this organization will become.

4. There is a balanced and equitable distribution of rewards.[9]

Servant leadership does not create servility. Here is what leads to many of the problems in the workplace and the world. The servant leader is not merely a doormat, doing whatever people ask, taking little or no initiative. Rather, the servant leader does several things that build people up and create a learning community: she is an *exegete*, looking into the body or community and saying what she sees, telling the truth about the organization. She is a *relational matchmaker*, making healthy connections between people, cultivating interdependence. She is a *shepherd of systems*, caring for the health and functioning of the structures, relationships, and subsystems. She is a *broker of gifts*, making connections between people and appropriate service opportunities. She is a *genetic counselor*, discovering the implications of the DNA of the organization, the origin and early history. She is a *playing coach*, participating as a player but offering encouragement. She is a *guide*, envisioning possible futures and leading the process of getting there. She is a *gardener*, cultivating those aspects of the organizational culture that are good and upbuilding, and allowing the weeds to wither and die. She is a *teacher*, asking more questions rather than always giving answers. Finally, she is a *trustee*, directing people to Jesus as head and King and leaving people dependent on God, not on the leader. But if being a kingdom leader involves being a servant of the Lord, it also involves caring for the whole person, including their souls.

Keeping Watch over the Flock 2: Kingdom Leadership Is Concerned with the Whole Person

The idea of having a "soul" is so deeply entrenched in Christian literature that we can barely read the Bible without misinterpreting what it means.

9. Block, *Stewardship*, xxi.

But in Hebrew thought we do not *have* a soul; we *are* one. In *The Complete Book of Everyday Christianity,* I offer these thoughts:

> In everyday conversation the word *soul* can mean at least two things: (1) a precious human person (as in "Two hundred souls were lost in the plane crash") and (2) the eternal or immortal part of a human being, an incorruptible core (as in "We commit the body to the grave knowing that she still lives in her soul"). We will see that the first is actually closer to biblical truth than the second (compare Acts 27:37 KJV with NIV). In the Bible *soul* and *spirit* are sometimes used interchangeably to speak of the interior of persons, especially in their longings for relationship with God. Add to this confusion one more word: the universal word *heart* as a metaphor for the motivating center of a person. This complex use of words reflects the contemporary confusion about what makes human beings "tick" and what constitutes a spiritual person.[10]

The idea that the soul is an immortal organ in the body, that tending to the soul is an eternal matter while attending to the body a temporal one, run so deep that to counter it seems almost heretical. But in the Bible the soul is not a part of or located within the body, to be released through death. It is part of the person, the longing part. More often than not, however, "soul" in the Old Testament does not refer to the spiritual/emotional part of a person that can be disconnected from bodily life. "Soul" refers to the person *as a longing person*[11]—longing for life, longing for God, longing for fruitfulness, longing for happiness. These are soul-person dimensions. So kingdom leadership is concerned with the whole person.

Soul Leadership Is Person Leadership

Life, for the biblical persons, is total and cannot be segmented into two parts: a disposable shell (the body) and an indestructible "spirit" core (the soul). Thus the familiar psalm, "Praise the Lord, O my soul; all my inmost being, praise his holy name" (103:1) could be simply and helpfully translated, "Bless the Lord, *O my life!*" Far from having three separate compartments, the human person is a psycho-pneuma-somatic (soul-spirit-body) unity. Touch a person's body and one has touched the person—a crucial Christian contribution to the matter of sexuality. We never "have" sex with

10. Stevens, "Soul."

11. Wolff, *Anthropology of the Old Testament*, 10, emphasis mine.

bodies but with souls, meaning persons! Touch the emotions and we touch persons. Touch the spirit and we have touched the whole person. In biblical anthropology we do not "have" a body, or soul, or spirit. We *are* a body, a soul, a spirit. And our ultimate hope in the kingdom of God after death is not as it was for the Greeks, the immortality of the soul, but the resurrection of the body (read the whole person).

So kingdom leadership is concerned not just about whether a person's soul has been saved, but also about the work people do and what that work means. Is it meaningful work expressing gifts and talents, contributing to loving our neighbors, or could a robot do it? Kingdom leadership is concerned for the context in which people work, the organizational culture. Is it toxic or empowering? Is it inhibiting of initiative or does it inspire self-determination, agency, and creativity? Kingdom leadership is concerned with empowerment. Is the workplace a dead-end situation or does it help people to grow and learn new skills? Kingdom leadership serves the followers. And in the process of giving leadership, and becoming a kingdom leader, in the hammer and heat of life, we grow spiritually.

Kingdom Leadership Is a Spiritual Discipline

I remember speaking years ago on the "Spirituality of Kingdom Leadership" and referring to spiritual disciplines that would be helpful, things about which I have written in my book *Seven Days of Faith*.[12] Included is the journey upward—such as prayer, fasting, Bible reading, and Bible meditation. Then there is the journey inward—such as retreating, silence, and walking through your life with Jesus and dealing with the hurts of your past, becoming aware of who you really are. And finally there is the journey outward—such as hospitality, service, corporate worship. But in fact, while these disciplines are helpful in forming a kingdom leader, *the leadership itself* is a spiritual discipline directing us Godward. To illustrate this let me tell you about my own experience.

The most influential person in my life has been—will you believe this?—my boss! Dr. Walter Wright was president of Regent College and asked me to become the academic dean. That's a story in itself as I do not have a PhD degree and have, in my life, largely run away from administrative roles. After a long process of meeting with the search committee and praying with my wife, I agreed to serve. Walter then said to me four things.

12. Stevens, *Seven Days of Faith*.

First, "I guarantee your success. If you fail it is because I have failed as your supervisor." Talk about empowerment! Second, "On your annual review there will be nothing negative. I will stay up late the night before we meet and write a long letter of affirmation." (I recall reading this and thinking, "Is this really me?") Third, "We will have breakfast every Thursday morning and when things are not going well we will deal with it right then, not on the annual review." The fourth was a big one. "In this job you will have to deal with yourself. You really like to teach. You get wonderful feedback from your students and it feeds something in you. But you are not going to get positive strokes in this job. Instead you will get a lot of criticism. And you will have to deal with yourself." Then he said something beautiful. "And I will help you," which he did in the hammer and heat of leadership. But this story includes one discipline that is conspicuously missing in the life of most kingdom leaders. That discipline is accountability.

I have heard many of the great preachers of the world and I normally cannot remember a thing they said. Except one. I heard Chuck Swindoll say that there was not one Christian leader in North America who fell who had an accountability group, a small group of people who knew what was going on inside and outside that leader. All who fell had followers, not peers. And it is peers we need. Mutual submission is a tough discipline.

The Need for Accountability

Kefa Sempagni was a person who became a Christian during the East Africa revival. During that revival people confessed their sins publicly against the backdrop of a great roar of praise and thanksgiving. But Kefa's confession personally turns me inside out.

> Hardly any of us can go to his own Christian community and say: "This is my body which is broken for you. I am laying all my professional skills, abilities, and economic resources at your disposal. Take them and use them as you see fit." We cannot do this, because we are not broken. We are too proud to give our lives away to people who are not perfect. We don't want to lose ourselves for sinners. We want to find the perfect person and the perfect community, but we never find them. So, like Judas, we make only a partial commitment to the body of believers to which we belong, and we find our identity in rebellion from them.[13]

---

13. Sempangi, "Walking in the Light," 25.

So Paul ends his final farewell with the Ephesian elders with these troubling words: "I know that after I leave, savage wolves will come in among you and will not spare the flock" (Acts 20:29). It turns out that there is an anti-kingdom at work, sometimes influencing us from outside, like wolves. But sometimes we are influenced by the wolves within. To this subject we now turn.

PART FIVE

Kingdom Resistance and the Kingdom Come

12

The Anti-Kingdom
in the Marketplace

"From the days of John the Baptist until now, the kingdom of heaven has
been subjected to violence, and violent people have been raiding it."

—JESUS, MATTHEW 11:12[1]

"When I feed the hungry they call me a saint. When I ask why the poor are
poor they call me a communist.

—COLUMBIAN PRIEST J. M. BONINO[2]

WORK IN THE WORLD is hard. We face a multilayered battle. We struggle
with people. But we also find resistance to the kingdom of God not just
from "flesh and blood struggles"—struggles with other human sinners—
but against "the rulers, against the authorities, against the powers of this
dark world and against the spiritual forces of evil in the heavenly realms."

1. This is admittedly a difficult verse. To provide context: John the Baptist has been
put in prison for his service in and to the kingdom of God. The Greek word *harpazo*
normally means "plunder" or "seize." There are two possible meanings to this phrase, the
first, that some of Jesus' followers and some of John's are trying to divert the mission of
Jesus into one of national liberation from Rome. But the more likely is that the violence
amounts to "the violent opposition encountered by 'the kingdom of heaven,' already seen
in the arrest and imprisonment of its herald, and more ominously foreshadowed in the
growing official opposition to Jesus himself." France, *Matthew*, 195.

2. Bonino, *Doing Theology in a Revolutionary Situation*, 44.

The "heavenly realms" are some of *the spiritual dimensions of the here and now* (Eph 6:12), loosely summarized under the rubric of "principalities and powers."

These powers range from structures and institutions (whether democracy, socialism, or capitalism), images that capture the imagination, traditions, right through to invisible spiritual beings, called demons and the devil himself (6:11) that are opposing God's rule. In Psalm 46 we have the famous sentence: "Be still, and know that I am God" (Ps 46:10). This is a good thing to do. Indeed in our attentional landscape where we are always "on," it is usually a good thing, indeed necessary, to turn off the TV, to fast from the internet to be available to God—which is a huge undertaking in this distracted world.[3] But this is *not* what the Psalm is about. God is speaking not primarily to us but to the powers. God says, "Be quiet. Leave off. Desist. Put down your weapons," just as Jesus spoke to the storm overtaking the boat and "rebuked the wind and the raging waters . . . and all was calm" (Luke 8:24). It is God addressing the storm. And there is a storm in the marketplace.

The View from the Ground

Jon Escoto is a business consultant in Manila and has worked for various multinational companies in the Philippines. He remarks on the magnitude and complexity of the problem, the anti-kingdom reality, he in his own country, and we, to some extent, face in the marketplace:

> Below are my observations on *how work goes* in my country, as validated by people I interface and breathe the same *business air* with.
>
> 1. Laborers' rights to minimum wages are thwarted excessively and continuously through the use of employment agencies or the justification that workers get free board and/or lodging.
>
> 2. Hopes of laborers for change in unjust working conditions are dampened by the formation of unions that are overly sympathetic to management.
>
> 3. Laborers' full productivity and owners' rights to the same are disregarded by professional managers' mental sloth and lack of passion.

3. See Crawford, *World Beyond Your Head.*

4. Laborers' and professional managers' rights to aspire to progressive and morally upright lives are blocked by owners' and policy makers' failure to follow the institution's vision and to be role models.

5. Laborers lose out in the end because of abusive labor leaders.

6. Employers' legitimate points of view are not listened to and labeled summarily as unjust.

7. Owners' rights to full disclosure and a fair return on their investments are consistently de-prioritized.

8. The environment is abused by starving marginalized groups or by never-satisfied capitalists.

9. Host communities are bled by institutions, yet abandoned for better locales, at early signs of decreasing profitability or inadequate budgets.

10. Host communities find themselves empty-handed when guest institutions leave, having failed to put up self-sustaining small industries.

11. Big suppliers are paid on time, while small suppliers are de-prioritized.

12. Products that are unsafe or not necessary are falsely advertised, "glamorized," and allowed to proliferate in the market.

13. Competition is so keen that competitors resort to below-the-belt tactics and unethical practices.

14. People in authority, both public and private, take advantage of their power to push whomever they can victimize to the limits.

15. Institutional problems are blown out of proportion because of politics and the sensationalistic media.

16. Professional managers and board members fight tooth and nail to usurp power and then preserve it, making decisions that damage the reputation and the lives of the institution, of families, friends, and even the general public.

17. Partnership agreements between and amongst local and foreign institutions that are one-sided abound.

18. Government regulations that are not well thought out or holistically encourage unethical practices.

19. Aids or grants that are not contextualized and holistic do not result in interventions that create sustainable or meaningful changes.

20. Graduates lack preparedness to take on even the first tier of work employment.

21. The poor get poorer, the middle class disappears, and the rich get richer.[4]

Briefly, this is the world, the flesh, and the devil. This handy outline of the three dimensions of resistance to the regal claims of God is found in the Anglican/Episcopal prayer book. One of the Collects (gathering prayers) is "Lord, we beseech thee, grant thy people grace to withstand the temptations of the world, the flesh, and the devil, and with pure hearts and minds to follow thee, the only God; through Jesus Christ our Lord."[5] These three dimensions of the anti-kingdom are a summary of what the Scripture describes.

Resistance from the "World"—Grappling with the Principalities and Powers[6]

Scripture uses *world* to describe the created order about which God could say, "it is very good" (Gen 1:31). But there was more than mere matter involved in making the world. God's creative activity involved placing humankind in a structured universe that included time (seven days), space (a sanctuary garden), relationships (covenant marriage and family), authorities, limits and structures (the tree of knowledge), and other creatures (animals and the serpent). Imagine a world without marriage, family, government, and without national borders (Acts 17:26)! All these are designed by God for our protection and for meaningful life. Bishop Lightfoot noted that this means we are living in a cosmos not a chaos. But *world* is also used to describe the world system that is now organized against God and his purposes[7] but which, nevertheless, God loves (John 3:16). There is some-

4. Jon Escoto was my student in a Theology of Work course in ATS-MBA program in Manila.

5. Collect, 18th Sunday after Trinity, *Anglican Prayer Book*, 247.

6. For a more extensive treatment of the powers, including many contemporary authors who deal with them, see Stevens, *Other Six Days,* 215–42. A few sections of this chapter were taken from that book.

7. John 14:17; 15:18, 19; 17:14, 15; 16:33; 1 John 2:15.

thing more to the opposition we face in the world than the mere sum of all the sinful attitudes and actions of people. It is systemic evil.

Jesus taught that the world cannot receive the Spirit (John 14:17), hates Jesus, and hates believers (15:18). Believers have been chosen "out of" the world (15:19) and are not "of" the world (17:14) even though they must live "in" the world (17:15). "In this world," Jesus says, "you will have trouble" (16:33). The Christian solution, as we will see, is not to be extricated from the world or, as was suggested by Gnostics to get the spirit/soul out of the physical body, but to live in this world wholeheartedly through the presentation of our bodily life to God (Rom 12:1–2), so being kept from both evil and the evil one (John 17:15). While the world sets out to conform us and shape us,[8] the Christian is called to be transformed (personally) and to become a transformer of society. We cannot do this as "separated" Christians. The place for a boat (a symbol of the people of God) is in the water (the world); water should not be in the boat. Yet, what one finds so frequently is a church claiming to free of the world but drawn up on the beach. When one looks in the boat, it is full of water!

Multifaceted Opposition

The trouble we experience in the world is multifaceted and comes to us through unjust or unloving structures, systems of business and finance, principles of conformity, social patterns, customs, and traditions that marginalize the life of the kingdom or positively oppose it. These are expressed by a cluster of biblical terms in the body of Paul's writings that include: *power/s, thrones, authorities, virtues, dominions, names,* and *thrones.*[9] When we translate this into our experience in the here and now it includes:

- Political, financial, juridical, and ecclesiastical rulers
- Traditions
- Images that grip our imagination
- Institutions that have become intractable
- Ideologies such as communism, capitalism, and socialism
- Structures/organizations

---

8. A lucid discussion of this is found in Berger, *Sacred Canopy*, chapter 1.

9. Rom 8:38; 1 Cor 15:24; Eph 1:21; 3:10; 6:12; Col 1:16; 2:10, 15.

- Mammon—money seen as our ultimate security
- Death that holds people in lifelong bondage
- The demonic and the devil himself

The powers in Scripture are centers of resistance ranging from structures to demonic beings. But here is the thing we often forget: the powers were created by Christ and for Christ (Col 1:16). They were originally good but have been colonized by Satan; they are fallen; they have taken on a life of their own and make godlike claims on us. But Christ overcame the powers, disarmed them, and showed their pretentious power through the cross (Col 2:13–15). In view of Christ's work, the theologian Oscar Cullmann compares the powers to "chained beasts" kicking themselves to death, still able to evince a threat and resistance but restrained—chained like the religion, culture, and government which put Jesus on to the cross with the title "King of the Jews" in three languages, Hebrew or Aramaic (religion), Greek (culture), and Latin (government). But Jesus overcame them through his resurrection and ascension.

Dealing with the Powers

In the marketplace we deal with the world which God loves but which is saturated with resistance to the reign of God. We face the almost idolatrous claims of the market, of capitalism, systemic evil, racism, cancel culture, and especially Mammon—the lure of money as our absolute and final security. How do we grapple with the principalities and powers? It depends. It depends on which power one is encountering. Sometimes the best strategy, with the Anabaptists, is suffering powerlessness. Sometimes the best strategy is to get in there as regents of our God and King and make a difference, as with the mainline Protestant denominations. Sometimes we respond with prayer and exorcism, as with charismatics. And occasionally, as with the liberation theologians of South America both Catholic and Protestant, we engage in civil disobedience and a just revolution. But in each case we do it through engagement in the kingdom rather than withdrawal from the world.

The second arena of resistance comes not from outside ourselves but inside: the flesh.

Resistance from the Flesh–Dealing with Human Nature Gone Astray

When Paul deals with "the flesh" he is normally not thinking that the location of our struggle is in our physical bodies. Indeed the "works [or acts] of the flesh" in Galatians 5:19–21 are almost all nonphysical. They deal with our emotional and spiritual orientation. "Flesh" means living and working as though Christ had not come, with humanity turned in on itself, living autonomously, being our own gods, in contrast with experiencing the fruit of the Spirit (Gal 5:22–23). While people tend to think of the acts of the flesh in terms of anthropology, it is really about eschatology, living in the old age rather than the new age of the kingdom of God that is the age of the Spirit. In the marketplace greed is rampant and one of the works of the flesh is "envy" (Gal 5:21).

The Anatomy of Greed

How does greed manifest itself? It generates discontentment with what we have. It nails our desires to the accumulation of things. It purports that we will find meaning in possessing things. It advertises that we will not be fulfilled without something more. It makes us love money. It makes us consider ourselves and others as mere consumers. And like lust, it attacks us in our imaginations. So it is a capital sin—in the head. The early church father Evagrios shows that it is not defined by purely material greed but "by the principle of *thinking about what does not yet exist*, a kind of preoccupation with imaginary and future things such as hopes and fears.[10] In the Ten Commandments it is called "covetousness" and it is the most inward of the Ten (Exod 20:17). So it is not easy to be in business, for example, or to be in marketing, without encountering greed.

I am always pleased when I hear of someone who is a follower of Jesus and is a graphic artist working in the advertising field. It is one place we should be. But it is not an easy assignment. Speaking as a professor of advertising history, Richard Pollay is fully aware of the dangers.

> Such intrusion, first into our consciousness and then into our inner voices, distracts us from the serenity of solitude and thereby

---

10. Jordan-Smith, "Seven (and more) Deadly Sins," 41 (emphasis his). Further development of the seven deadly sins and the fruit of the Spirit is found in Stevens and Ung, *Taking Your Soul to Work*.

inhibits self-awareness. The repetitive, fantastic, one-sided and often exhortative rhetorical styles of advertising combine to blur the distinction between reality and fantasy, producing a state of uncritical consciousness, passivity and relative powerlessness. Non-wants become wants; wants become needs.[11]

My first cousin was the national sales manager for a large furniture company. His sales ethic was simply this: "I will only sell to someone who meets all three requirements: they want it, they need it and they can afford it." The Puritan William Perkins offers in his "Treatise on Callings" some ways of dealing with covetousness.

(1) We must labor to see our particular situation as a providence of God no matter how difficult;

(2) We must resolve in our conscience that God is our portion (Ps 16:6);

(3) We must resolve not to seek more in this world than we actually need—we have no warrant to pray for abundance.[12]

We deal with the flesh by mortification (nailing our evil desires to the cross of Christ) and aspiration (breathing in the Holy Spirit). Speaking to the "flesh" and the "Spirit," Paul does not consider them the higher and lower human nature, but the orientation of our person, work, and service, either to the old age, without Christ, or to the new age, the age of the Spirit. "Those who belong to Christ Jesus have crucified the flesh with its passions and desires. Since we live by the Spirit, let us keep in step with the Spirit" (Gal 5:24–5). But the most sinister of resisters is yet to come.

Resistance from the Devil and Demons—Personal Spiritual Beings Opposed to the Kingdom of God

Some resistance comes from personal spiritual beings that have intelligence and will, capable of purposeful activity but determined to oppose the rule of God. Representing the cosmic perspective of the New Testament authors, Heinrich Schleir speaks of

Satan and his hordes, those manifold developments and effusions of the spirit of wickedness with their combination of intelligence

11. Pollay and Stevens, "Advertising," 26.

12. Perkins, *Works of That Famous Minister,* 770C.

and lust for power, exist by influencing the world and mankind in every sector and at all levels, and by making them instruments and bearers of their powers. There is nothing on earth which is absolutely immune from their power. They can occupy the human body, the human spirit, what we call "nature," and even the forms, bearers and situations of history. Even religions, including the Christian teaching, can become tools of their activity. Their spirit penetrates and overwhelms everything.[13]

A number of popular novels and treatments of spiritual warfare, notably the works of Frank Peretti and David Watson, essentially take this approach. A more scholarly approach is taken by Clinton Arnold in *Powers of Darkness: Principalities and Powers in Paul's Letters*. But taken to the extreme these authors define the problem of the Christian too narrowly. The devil is not behind every resistance. They reduce mission to intercession and exorcism. There is little left we can do, little for which we are responsible.

The Cost of Losing the Demonic

Having said this, we must accept the important corrective offered by those who warn, as John Stott did, that in locating the powers in structures we have lost the demonic. *Western society has largely rejected the spiritual interpretation of life.* Even the church turns to social analysis to find out what is going on, and leaves the spiritual realities behind and within the visible and present. Years ago James Stewart traced the intellectual history of this demise of our biblical framework in these brilliant words:

> St. Paul's "principalities and powers"—the "spirit forces of evil" whose malignant grip upon the souls of men called forth "a second Adam to the fight and to the rescue"—are now known, we are told, to have been mere apocalyptic imagination. To this result Newton, Darwin and Freud certainly contributed. For Newton's work left no room for an irrational principle in nature; and the devil is essentially irrational, teleologically indefinable—as St. John marks by his significant use of *anomia* and St. Paul by the phrase "the mystery of iniquity" (1 John 3.4). . . . Darwin's picture of the biological struggle for existence was hailed as radically superseding the Biblical picture of the cosmic struggle between the demons and the kingdom of the Lord. Finally, Freud banished the powers

13. Schleir, *Principalities and Powers in the New Testament*, 28–29.

of darkness from their last stronghold, the soul, by successfully dissolving them into psychological complexes, neuroses, and the like: so that the good fight of faith becomes simply a matter of inner individual adjustment.[14]

Embodying this last modern viewpoint accurately, Walter Wink states, "We moderns cannot bring ourselves by any feat of will or imagination to believe in the real existence of these mythological entities that traditionally have been lumped under the category 'principalities and powers.'"[15] Yet to be biblical Christians we must be converted to that which we may not be easily convinced about. As indicated in the survey of biblical words above, the Christian in the world must deal comprehensively with what we face. And Scripture witnesses to the complexity of systemic evil: structures, spiritual hosts, angels and demons, the devil, and the last enemy, death (1 Cor 15:24–27)—all arenas of spiritual warfare. Even to speak of the "spirituality" of institutions, as does Wink,[16] does not fully represent the complexity of evil encountered in the world. A truly biblical theology of the powers must include the Gospels where Jesus clearly is encountering evil spiritual beings (Luke 9:1) as well as structures. So in reality many of the seemingly autonomous powers are being influenced by Satan himself. The powers have been colonized—influenced and controlled by a foreign power. And in some cases the alien power (Satan) has "home rule."

The Complexity of Evil

The complex vision of the last book of the Bible reveals multiple (and systemically interrelated) levels of difficulty that can be pictured as concentric circles of influence: the red dragon (Satan) at the center of it all (Rev 12); the two beasts (13) representing diabolical authority and diabolical supernaturalism—a larger circle; the harlot (17) representing the sum total

14. Stewart, *Faith to Proclaim*, 76–77.

15. Wink, *Naming the Powers*, 4.

16. Wink maintains that "the 'principalities and powers' are the inner and outer aspects of any given manifestation of power. As the inner aspect they are the spirituality of institutions, the 'within' of corporate structures and systems, the inner essence of outer organizations of power. As the outer aspect they are political systems, appointed officials, the 'chair' of an organization, laws—in short, all the tangible manifestations which power takes" (*Naming the Powers*, 5). Wink, however, in line with others who want to demythologize Paul's language, frankly states his presupposition that we moderns cannot bring ourselves to believe in "mythological entities."

of pagan culture and (in the outermost ring) Babylon (18) as the world system. This elaborate picture shows that the Christian in the world not only encounters a multifaceted opposition but one in which there are interdependently connected dimensions. The Revelation shows us that the political power of Romans 13, the good servant of God in Paul's day, has become in Revelation 13 the instrument of Satan (in this case the same government but more colonized and corrupted)—thus showing the way in which supernatural and nonhuman forces and personages may influence and corrupt human institutions, structures, and patterns of cultural and social life. At the center of the concentric circles is the archenemy of the King and kingdom—Satan.

Michael Green outlines four biblical convictions:

1. There is a supreme anti-God force called the devil or Satan.

2. Satan has demonic allies that afflict human beings.

3. Jesus came to free people from these forces.

4. Jesus empowered his followers to do this liberating work.

He gives this wise advice: "Do not attempt this ministry alone, when you are not full of the Holy Spirit, and do not get hooked on it. Do not seek it. Do not be surprised by it."[17]

Jesus encountered the devil at the beginning of his ministry. The three testings by Satan into which he was led by the Holy Spirit are arenas where we ourselves are tested by Satan in the workplace: provision—"turn these stones into bread"; pleasure—"throw yourself down from the pinnacle of the temple because it is written, 'you will not strike your foot against a stone'"; and power—"All this I will give you if you will bow down and worship me."[18]

For the first year of our decade in East Africa I attached myself to a mature pastor. In the course of visiting home after home, I asked Canon Mangaya, "Do you cast out demons?" "No, never," he responded. I was taken aback. Then he said, "Jesus does." "Tell me more," I said. He responded, "When we know there is a problem two of us go to a home and pray that Jesus will deal with the problem. Then we go back the next day to see what Jesus has done." Sublime. How else does God speak to the powers today?

17. See Green, *Evangelism in the Early Church*, 189.

18. These three temptations are elaborated in the second edition of *Seven Days of Faith*, 137–60.

Speaking to the Powers Today

Psalm 46 starts with an amazing word of encouragement. "God is our refuge and strength, an ever-present help in trouble" (46:1). Three times it is said in the Psalm that God protects us as a refuge and a fortress (vv. 7, 11). First, there is protection. There is, second, help and strength: "an ever-present help." Refuge is external; strength is internal to empower the weak for action. There are two wonderful images of God in Psalm 46. First, there is the castle, the refuge, or the protecting fortress. But the second image is of a river that brings life and energy (v. 4). "There is a river whose streams make glad the city of God, the holy place where the Most High dwells. God is within her, she will not fall; God will help her at the break of day." Here, in the midst of struggle, attacks, seductions, tumults both outside and inside, there is a source of life, a source of sustenance—provision. The obvious reference is to Jerusalem but not just the city itself, since the city was without running water and Hezekiah had to cut a channel through solid rock to bring water in from the spring of Gihon outside the wall.

The picture of God's help is a quiet supply of water in a city besieged. I have a medieval theological map of the world that has Jerusalem in the center of everything. It has a biblical basis. In the prophet Ezekiel's vision of the end times when there is the fulfilment of the whole human story, he pictures an ideal Jerusalem with a river flowing from the throne of God in the temple with trees on each side that bear fruit monthly, and the leaves of the trees are for the healing of the nations. And the prophet is invited to walk in that river. He goes deeper and deeper, covering ankles, waist, and chest. So we are invited to walk into the renewing, refreshing stream of the kingdom of heaven.

This image of the river that makes glad the city of God points to the kingdom of heaven, God's abode. And in the last book of the New Testament, this river appears again as flowing from the new Jerusalem with the tree of life on either side and the leaves of the tree are for the healing of the nations. This is a picture of heaven, the fulfilment of the kingdom of God. Heaven is where life comes from. And amazingly, when someone like C. S. Lewis says that the people who lived for the next life were the most helpful to this world, he is saying that those oriented to the center of God's rule and love (here pictured as a city and a river) are able to do what is really important in this world. It was heavenly minded people who effectively led the movement to abolish the English slave trade. Heavenly minded people started hospitals, hospices, universities, rescued abandoned babies from the garbage dumps of Rome. Heavenly minded people raised the status of women as not being second class.

Yes, protection and provision are in the kingdom. But there is, in the third place, a presence: "ever-present" help.

For none of the above protection and provision could happen if God were absent or impersonal like a force. Paul ends his treatment of the armor of God with a call to prayer. "And pray in the Spirit on all occasions with all kinds of prayers and requests" (Eph 6:18). Prayer is simply friendship with God, attending to God, being with God who is ever present. God is present in whatever challenges personally, socially, spiritually, and relationally we are facing, indeed God is present in government, in the media, and in the workplace.

In 1985 Gail and I were training underground pastors in the old Soviet Union. I was taking her picture below the Kremlin and a man spoke to me gruffly, or so I thought. Perhaps, I thought, he considered that I was taking his picture without his permission. But when I explained that I was taking my wife's picture he said, in perfect English, "No, I want you to take a picture of me and my friend." I did and then he said, "Are you a Christian?" I had been warned against answering this question. But the Spirit led me to say, "Yes." And then I asked him if he was. He said, "Yes" and then took out from his pocket an icon of Jesus and recited Psalm 51 from perfect memory. I asked who he was. He explained that he was the top government filmmaker in Russia and that he put into his films as much as he could of the gospel of Jesus. We went into a church, lit some candles, and prayed together. God provides ever-present help.

Where isn't God?

A personal, protecting, and providing God can enable us to grapple with the powers of resistance that we face in the workplace, and everywhere else. "God is our refuge and strength, an ever present help in trouble. Therefore we will not fear."

A further resource for the kingdom ministry and mission is the people of God, the church, to which subject we now turn.

13

So What about the Church?

The Kingdom People

"We are not sent to preach the church but to announce the kingdom."

—MORTIMER ARIAS[1]

"If the church is to impart to the world a message of hope, love,
faith, justice and peace, something of this should be visible
and tangible in the church itself."

—DAVID J. BOSCH[2]

THE CHURCH AND THE kingdom are not the same thing but a lot of people
think that this is the case! In *The Kingdom of God*, Old Testament scholar
John Bright says, "There is no tendency in the New Testament to identify
the visible church with the Kingdom of God."[3] But the relationship of the
church to the kingdom of God is critically important. The church is a visible outcropping of the kingdom, a resource when we are facing resistance
in the marketplace, and a sign of hope that the kingdom has come and
is coming. The church, as Charles Ringma says, is a sign, sacrament, and
servant of the kingdom. It is important to unpack this trilogy of meanings.

1. Arias, *Announcing the Reign of God*, 118.
2. Bosch, *Transforming Mission*, 414.
3. Bright, *Kingdom of God*, 236.

Why? The church has in so many ways lost its purpose for being in the world other than to win people for Christ and to advance the church itself. One of the problems of the church today is that it is concerned to "bring in the church" rather than to "bring in the kingdom." We bring in the church through church growth, church planting, and outreach, all good things in themselves. But how does the church bring in the kingdom? And how does the marketplace figure in the equation?

The Church and the Kingdom in the West and North

Many people today in the north and west of the globe have given up on the church (not so in Africa and in much of Asia). I was once asked to attend a faculty retreat and to comment on the culture in which we are serving in the West. I said, we are *post*-Christendom (which means we cannot count on the culture or state to reinforce our faith), *post*modern (which means there is supposedly no absolute truth, only your truth and my truth), *post*-Christian (which means society is truly secularized or desecrated), and *post*-church (which means many true Christians have given up on the church, what the British poet and critic Algernon Charles Swinburne described in these haunting words: "I could worship the crucified if he did not come to me with his leprous bride, the church").[4] But finally I suggested to the faculty that today, in the West, we have *post-Christian Christians* (meaning that some are true followers of Jesus but will not associate themselves with the name *Christian*.) Such people are more inclined to view themselves in relationship with the kingdom of God but not to the church—wrongly, I maintain, and I will seek to expound why.

The relationship of the church to the kingdom is a vexed one. Recently, focusing on the *people* dimension of the kingdom in his book *Kingdom Conspiracy: Returning to the Radical Mission of the Local Church*, Scot

---

4. I have been unable to locate the exact origin of these words though they have been in my personal notes for years. Swinburne was born in 1837. His biographer, Glen Everett, notes, "His treatment of Christianity seems a characteristically idiosyncratic one—that is, although he delighted in opposing organized religion and savagely attacked the Roman Catholic Church for its political role in a divided Italy, he makes detailed use of biblical allusion, though often for blasphemous ends. Although Algernon turned to nihilism while at Oxford, he never became indifferent to religion, as "Hymn to Proserpine" and "Hertha" make clear." Charles Swinburne is famous for one line in his poem "Hymn to Proserpine" ("Thou hast conquered, O pale Galilean; the world has grown grey from thy breath").

McKnight argues that "kingdom" describes the *people* governed by King Jesus. All we see is an inauguration of that kingdom creating a tension between kingdom now and kingdom not yet. But "church" describes the very same realities, now in a mixed and somewhat messy way, not yet in its final purity.[5] But McKnight's emphasis on *the kingdom as people* misses the dynamic dimension of the kingdom, the fact that it is God's active government in the world, not just in the gathered and the scattered life of the church. So when McKnight says, "Kingdom mission is church mission, church mission is kingdom mission, and there is no kingdom mission that is not church mission"[6] he has equated the church to the kingdom *as people*—exclusively. But the kingdom is *people, place, and presence*. It is where our Lord rules dynamically, as shown in the final reign of God in the new heaven and new earth: a people, a place, and the presence of God.

McKnight does, however, rightly indicate through this equation that the church is called not to "bring in" the church but to bring in the kingdom, if not as extensively as McKnight presumably believes. In reviewing the book one reader notes: "His bottom line is that any work, however socially beneficial or morally laudable, that isn't tied directly to the Church and done with the sole express purpose of bringing people to Christ is not kingdom work. And one is left with the impression, intended or not, that by 'the Church' he means exclusively the institutional church."[7] So I am left with the summary of my colleague, Charles Ringma, who says, "The kingdom of God is all of God's upholding, renewing, and fulfilling activity in the world and we are invited to participate in this, witness to it, and rejoice in its manifestations." Ringma continues, "The church birthed in the kingdom is to reflect the kingdom of God and to invite others into its embrace. In doing this the church is a sign, servant, and sacrament of the kingdom of God."[8] We need now to unpack Ringma's trilogy of the relation of the church to the kingdom.

5. McKnight, "Church and Kingdom," 38. McKnight points out that it is unfair to compare the church now with the kingdom having fully come, that the church is both now and yet to come, just as is the kingdom.

6. McKnight, "Church and Kingdom," 38.

7. Grayson, "Faith Meets World."

8. Email to the author, February 10, 2021.

The Church as Sign of the Kingdom

The church does not exist for itself. It is not the body (of Christ) beautiful, a system exclusively for being but rather a system of *being and doing* purposively planted in this age as a sign of something that is coming and really beautiful: the kingdom of God. As we have seen the kingdom is concerned with the flourishing of all human life, enterprise, and the creation. The church is part of the kingdom but exists as sign that the end has begun to come, that heaven has begun to come to earth. The church is a sign that the "renewal of all things," something Jesus spoke about (Matt 19:28), has started, and started especially with the rejuvenation of persons, called "new birth" in John's Gospel and in some of the letters. Here is one way of visualizing the "sign" function of the church.

When road planners try to put a highway through a hill they usually do not run the road up and down the hill but rather cut *through* it so the road can remain fairly level. But in doing so they reveal all the strata of both sides of the cut: bedrock at the bottom, gravel, sand, and topsoil. What we see as we drive through such a cut is only the outcropping. But the outcropping is a sign that there is a lot more, though not immediately visible. So in its life together the church has embraced the values and virtues of the kingdom, demonstrates the power of God to bring renewal, and points to the reality now somewhat invisible, that God is at work in the world bringing human flourishing, true humanity, and renewal. Let me suggest some of the ways that the church serves as signs of the kingdom:

- The church is itself a sign of the renewal of people and of everything. People who become companions in the kingdom (Rev 1:9) have experienced new life, new birth, new wine, and the new age. This is not to say that the people in the church are perfect. But they are being saved, being transformed, and being transfigured (2 Cor 3:18). They become a sign of the kingdom coming. Even the way that Christians die with the certain hope of resurrection is a sign of the kingdom come and coming.

- The church brings together people from different races, backgrounds, rich and poor alike, and with other boundary-breaking inclusions that portend to the ultimate community in the new heaven and new earth, when every language, race, and people group will be one though not merged. This is true because the cross of Christ has broken down the wall that separates people (Eph 2:14–17). The church is not a "you-all" club composed of people who speak with the same twang and who would gather anyway.

- The church is a worshipping community not only in its liturgy but in worshipping God in life seven days a week. As mentioned above, if someone would not want to be worshipping God 24/7 they would not want to be in the universal presence of God in the new heaven and new earth.

- The church is a community of love. Of course, the church does not have a monopoly on love and because it is composed of sinners in the process of being saved it is sometimes fractious and less than loving. But it is a remarkable community. "See how these Christians love one another" was said of the early Christians and is often said today when people hear of casseroles delivered to the sick, providing personal care, visiting the prisoner, undertaking the needs of widows, and taking in orphans.

- The church is a community of joy. Joy is more than happiness, at least happiness as circumstantially informed. It is the distinguishing mark of the Christian life as suggested in the New Testament, so that people were able to greet one another with the phrase, "Joy be to you" (Acts 15:23).[9]

So the church is a pointer, a sign. It is a public pole of response to the regal claims of Jesus. It witnesses to the fact that God is at work bringing renewal and new life. But the church is not merely a sign. It is also a sacrament of the kingdom of God.

The Church as Sacrament of the Kingdom

Orthodox theologian Alexander Schmemann says the church is the "sacrament—the gift, the beginning, the presence, the promise, the reality, the anticipation of the Kingdom."[10] The word *sacrament* comes from the Latin *sacramentum*, which means a military oath of obedience made by soldiers, though the word has more commonly been used for certain rites and ceremonies in Christian worship. But the most common definition of

9. Jas 1:1; 2 Cor 13:11; Luke 1:28; Matt 28:9; Phil 3:1; 4:4; 4:10; 3 John 4. See further Barclay, *Flesh and Spirit*, 76–83.

10. Schmemann, *For the Life of the World*, 113.

a sacrament is attributed to Augustine, which is summed up in the *Book of Common Prayer* as an "outward and visible sign of an inward and spiritual grace."[11] In an excellent article on the subject, C. O. Buchanan notes how the liturgical and ecumenical movements have recovered a dimension of church sacramental life that was present in the sixteenth-century discussion of "how many sacraments are there?" He points out that the recipients who received the sacraments, whether two in the Protestant tradition or seven in the Catholic tradition, are affirming "their calling to fulfil the loving, peace-making, missionary and other tasks of God in the world."[12] Strangely this brings us back to the original Latin meaning of *sacramentum*, a military or missional oath! But the church does not only celebrate the sacraments; it *is* a sacrament, a means of grace in the world.

That means the church is an *effective* sign outwardly of an inward and spiritual grace in the world. That is, the church—not the building of course, but the people—brings grace into the world and that by the people living and working under the influence of the head, Jesus Christ. The missiologist Lesslie Newbigin proposes that while the church normally situates itself near where people sleep (in their homes) it needs to be present in the workplace as a church. He makes the radical proposal that "The church must be where workers are, speak the language they speak, inhabit the worlds they inhabit." He offers several practical proposals. The gathering should be at or near the workplace, must be local in the cultural sense, and local in its leadership structures. "These fellowship groups should be effectively promoted to the status of full-fledged congregations where the Word is preached and the sacraments fully and rightly administered." In doing so the church becomes a means of grace in society.[13]

Even without being situated other than where people sleep—something, sad to say, that is rarely done—the church is a means of grace bringing renewal, hope, and flourishing. Has the church always done this? Of course not. It is a community of sinners being saved. But has the church done the world any good? Has it brought grace, spiritual help, and hope into the world? Yes, remarkably, century after century. Even today students, staff, and faculty of the Asian Theological Seminary in Manila are bringing to prisons grace and help, including food, masks, and hope during the COVID-19 pandemic. A Canadian pastor in 1930 reviewed the entire

11. Buchanan, "Sacrament."

12. Buchanan, "Sacrament," 607.

13. Quoted in Kaemingk, "Lesslie Newbigin's Missional Approach," 326.

history of the church in the Western world in its social and spiritual contribution—hospitals, hostels, burying the dead during plagues, starting
universities, providing relief during famines and natural disasters, just to
mention a few—and concludes that we have done our best work in history
as a pioneer, not merely an ambulance caring for the weak and victimized.[14]

The very life of the church makes the church a sacrament for the world.
In a sense we bring Sunday into Monday. In so doing the church brings
grace into the world even through its liturgy. "Liturgy" literally means "the
work of the people." But this work is worship. Monks speak of their liturgy
as the "work of God" or *opus dei*. Sometimes they do so in a dualistic way,
considering the work their do in the fields and kitchens to be lesser work.
But by devoting themselves to the worship of God with their whole beings,
as ordinary worshippers do in their whole-life worship, they express something profound, namely that all of bodily life is meant to be, as Paul said,
in Romans 12:1–2, presented to God as a living sacrifice that "is your true
and proper worship." Schmemann calls the Eucharist (Communion) "the
preface of the world to come, the door into the kingdom. . . . At the same
time [the Eucharist] asserts that when we proclaim the kingdom *which is to
come*, we affirm that God *has already endowed us with it.*"[15] In doing so we
declare that everything is sacred, loaded with grace and the glory of God.
Everything is either sacred or desecrated—not secular.

Theologian Hans Boersma says this:

> Sacramental language recognizes both the real presence of God
> in our earthly, time-space realities and the infinite transcendence
> of the mystery that is the triune God himself. This sacramental
> participation will reach its perfection in the New Jerusalem, which
> John describes as a "new heaven and a new earth" (Rev. 21:1).[16]

The Jewish theologian Abraham Heschel speaks of the Sabbath this
same way. For Heschel, the Sabbath is "the presence of God's reign on
earth." So, says Joshua Sweeden, "The Lord's Day is a celebration of the
curse undone. In Christ the new creation has begun and restoration breaks
into time."[17]

So in multiple ways the church is a sacrament of the kingdom. It does
this through its prayerful intercession for what is going on in the world. It

14. Oliver, *Social Achievements of the Christian Church.*

15. Schmemann, *For the Life of the World*, 39.

16 Boersma, *Heavenly Participation*, 187.

17. Sweeden, *Church and Work*, 113. Heschel is also quoted here.

does this through its corporate worship, which points to the inward and spiritual grace God is bringing to the world. It does this through the work that its members do, their worship-work (liturgy) when they are not gathered. It does this as an indication of where things are ultimately going: the transfiguration of the world into the kingdom of God. And it does this, as we now see, by being servant of the kingdom.

The Church as Servant of the Kingdom

In Howard Snyder's *Community of the King*, he offers two vitally important statements. First, God's master plan is the restoration of his creation (people and "all things," Eph 1:10). "The redemption of persons is the center of God's plan, but it is not the circumference of that plan."[18] But the second is this. The church in God's plan "is more than God's agent for evangelism; it is, in submission to Christ, the agent of God's entire cosmic purpose."[19] Here is the distinction between bringing in the church and bringing in the kingdom. How does this happen?

Individually the people are in the world (in the dispersed life of the church) serving, witnessing, doing compassionate work, performing kingdom work in the marketplace, making a difference in education, politics, and art. In so doing they are engaged in kingdom work. They do this, as we have seen above, through witness (verbal and nonverbal), by their whereabouts and by their work. The church is a rhythm of gathering and dispersion. In the dispersed life the people are seeded, planted, and immersed in the world. They are penetrating and salting society. Jesus used an abundance of penetration images for the kingdom: salt, light, yeast, seeds, keys, and fire. But what about the corporate life?

It is critically important that each local church assist its members to be empowered for their full-time service to God and neighbor in the workplace. I am calling this a tool kit for pastors and church leaders to assist members for their ministry in bringing the kingdom into the whole universe (Eph 4:10). Here are ten tools.

A tool to be used in corporate worship (Sunday or Saturday): Interviewing every week or each month a person who works in the world Monday to Friday and praying for them.

---

18. Snyder, *Community of the King*, 48.
19. Snyder, *Community of the King*, 55.

A tool to be used by small groups: Connecting small group Bible study with Sunday sermons, especially when you are doing a series on work, service, or vocational discernment. Using published Bible study guides in small groups that cover work and service. E.g., *Service* (InterVarsity Press), *The Search for Satisfying Work* (Harold Shaw Publishers).

Seminar tools in the local church: Offering short seminars focusing on aspects of work life using members as presenters. For example, "Whose Work Matters to God," "Discerning Your Calling," and "Taking Your Soul to Work." IMT, the Institute for Marketplace Transformation, has samples of these seminars. Contact registrar@imtglobal.org.

Christian education tools in the local church: Consider a Sunday school class on work. The "Doing God's Business" films 1 and 2 can be used with this. The films and the study guides for discussion are available free from https://imtglobal.org.

Staffing tools: Larger churches can employ a staff person to be marketplace pastor, encouraging people in their integration of faith and work, visiting and mentoring people in the workplace, running seminars and classes for integration. Smaller churches can draw into leadership a retired person who is self-employed or working as a volunteer to be a marketplace pastor or a marketplace coach. This person could also minister to youth in the area of vocational discernment and seeing that all good occupations are arenas for serving God and neighbor.

Communication tools: When church directories are printed or put online, and with the permission of the people, name their occupation.

Pastoral care tools: Church leaders can visit people in the workplace for a minimum of two hours, possibly longer, offering to pray silently for them when they are there and visiting over coffee breaks or lunches, discussing the way their work is a ministry, issues they face, and what difference their faith makes to how they handle these. If a pastor were to spend a half day every week in the workplace of members there could be extensive learning on the part of the pastor and the worker as well as positive encouragement for the worker.

Commissioning tools: When people have a proven ministry in the workplace or some arena of out-of-church engagement they can be publicly commissioned to this ministry in a Sunday service or a church gathering using resources that are available through IMT.

Networking tools: Monthly or biweekly noon-hour or breakfast gatherings of people working in the same geographical area can accomplish extraordinary one-another ministry and mutual upbuilding for ministry in the workplace.

Vocational discernment tools: The local church is the best context in which persons can discern their callings since we have some idea of *who* is calling and what the calling of God means to people. This can be done through youth programs, through Sunday school youth and adult classes, through children's programs, and through occasional seminars with hands-on exercises, such as the seminar offered by IMT.[20]

But there is a further way the church can be the servant of the kingdom. It is this: by creating kingdom consciousness so that the people of God can see signs of the kingdom coming, celebrate that, and pray that the kingdom will indeed come more and more.

The church is sign, sacrament, and servant of the kingdom of God. As John Bright says, "The New Testament Church is the people of the Kingdom of God."[21] In so being and doing the church's life and work is an acted prayer, "Your kingdom come." The big thing for the church to do is not to bring in the church, but to be a sign, sacrament, and servant of the kingdom of God.

---

20. The Pastor's Toolbox is available from the Institute for Marketplace Transformation. Contact registrar@imtglobal.org.

21. Bright, *Kingdom of God*, 242–43.

14

Working Our Way to Heaven

"The only ultimate disaster that can befall us, I have come to realize,
is to feel ourselves to be at home here on earth."

—Malcolm Muggeridge[1]

"All who have committed their work in faithfulness to God will be by Him
raised up to share in the new age, and will find that their labor was not lost,
but that it has found its place in the completed kingdom."

—Lesslie Newbigin[2]

"This gospel of the kingdom will be preached in the whole world
as a testimony to all nations, and then the end will come."

—Jesus, Matthew 24:14

I ADMIT THE TITLE of this chapter is provocative, especially for a Protestant
who, like Luther, protested against the idea that we could get to heaven by
good works. But, of course, it is not just in the church at the time of Luther
that this idea abounded, namely that we get to heaven by a human achieve-
ment, by saying prayers, giving alms, or serving in the church. It is with
us today. And, incidentally, Luther actually wrote a brilliant essay on good

1. Muggeridge, *Jesus Rediscovered*, 17–18.
2. Quoted in Sherman, *Kingdom Calling*, 236.

works. But I also admit that I borrowed the title from one of my favorite Roman Catholic authors, Cardinal Stephan Wyszynski, a Polish author who was mentor to the late Pope John Paul II. His *All You Who Labor: Work and the Sanctification of Daily Life* was originally entitled in translation *Working Your Way to Heaven*.[3] It is a great title in spite of the possible overtones, or undertones. I want to take the title seriously. Will some of the work we did in this life last and find its place in the next life? And will we be working in the new heaven and new earth, or will be just sitting around singing the same worship song endlessly?

The Grand Finale of the Kingdom Come

There is a new world coming but it is even better than what the bank proposed in the Vancouver airport Jetway. It has begun to come now, for the kingdom of God is now. But it is also not yet. It is here like salt in the meat and yeast in the dough, but not fully here. That indeed is the mystery of the kingdom of God. But it is not a secret.

The mystery is now revealed by the teaching, works, and person of Jesus. So what will it look like when the kingdom comes fully at the end of history, when Christ returns and there is the grand finale of the human story on earth? The world will not end with a fizzle or a bang, but the grand rendezvous with Jesus in his second coming, the resurrection of the dead, the final judgment of everyone, the inauguration of the new heaven and new earth, and the consummation of the kingdom of God. These are like five mountain peaks in North America that early explorers traveling west would see in the Rocky Mountains. They would be able to identify the five peaks but not be able to see which one comes first, second, and so on. So there is a future and a glorious one at that, but the exact order is somewhat uncertain, at least from our present perspective.

The last book in the Bible, Revelation, is about the King and the kingdom. Its vision and the surrounding events around the vision is summarized in this verse: "The kingdom of the world has become the kingdom of our Lord and of his Messiah, and he will reign for ever and ever" (Rev 11:15). It is a fantastic book, and the first one I read the night I became a follower of Jesus. It is in a genre of literature that does not exist today: apocalyptic. The Apocalypse of John (Revelation) ushers us into a world of

---

3. Wyszynski, *All You Who Labor.* The author writes in chapter 11 about the "Mystery of Redemption in Work" and "Work as an Instrument of Salvation."

dragons, beasts, angels, cosmic catastrophes, and martyrs chanting hymns. We are swept from one riveting vision to the next, transported from heaven to earth and back again, in an upstairs-downstairs drama. Bowls of judgment are poured out on the earth while cringing multitudes call on hills to cover them from the wrath of the Lamb. There is a final battle, a wonderful wedding supper, and an exquisite garden city.

Apocalypse was to the first century what science fiction is to the twenty-first century. Imagine trying to explain science fiction to a first-century tentmaker in Ephesus, or apocalypse to a cabdriver in Boston or Hong Kong today. Comparisons may, however, be made. The Revelation of John can be compared with a dissolve-fade slide show—the Lion dissolves into a Lamb standing as though slain—a drama organized in dramatic form with overlapping sequences of seven seals, trumpets, and bowls, with the major pastoral messages offered at the moments of maximum dramatic intensity—or a symphony—it has more songs than all the rest of the New Testament. But none of these comparisons does justice to the unique form of literature that flourished between 200 BC and AD 100. The apostle John is unquestionably an apocalyptist.[4]

Who would want to read it? What would they gain by reading it?

It was written to seven churches in the Roman province of Asia, modern Turkey. Some of these churches were being seduced by a friendly culture and some were being persecuted by a hostile culture—not unlike churches today. Now, you would not throw a poem to a person drowning in the water. But if someone were drowning in meaninglessness, a poem or an apocalypse might be just the thing. And this book is just the thing. It provisions the faith of the people through imagination. It sneaks into our souls as an art form. It takes the veil off everyday life to show us how the world looks to a person in the Spirit. At the same time it gives us a vision of the final end. And the end is beautiful and terrible, beautiful as a wedding and terrible as a wake. It is terrible because all opposition to the rule of God, all the forces and personages of evil have to be finally dealt with, and beautiful as there is the grand rendezvous with Jesus, the final communion of the people of God with their Lord and King Jesus. This turns out to be the final union of heaven and earth. Read chapter 19, where the wedding and the wake take place by the one who is "King of kings and Lord of lords" (19:16). The kingdom has fully come. This is the new world having fully arrived.

---

4. See Stevens, "Poems for People in Distress." Some of the foregoing was excerpted from this article.

Eden Transfigured

So we are then ushered in Revelation 21 and 22 into a final vision not of Eden restored, but the garden of Eden transfigured as the context for the new Jerusalem, the final living quarters and workplace of all the people of God. In what is arguably the best renewal verse in the Bible, Jesus, sitting on the throne of God, says, "I am making everything new!" (21:5). This is not a brand-new creation, as though God will annihilate everything in the world when Christ returns, as some wrongly interpret the somewhat enigmatic words of the apostle Peter (2 Pet 3:10–13). Indeed this passage ends with our looking forward to a new (really renewed) heaven and a new (renewed) earth (2 Pet 3:13). We dare not drop the new earth from the phrase. So the two questions we ask about our work in this life and the next find their answer partly in this last, strange book of the New Testament. Here are the questions we ask about it.

First, will any of our work done in this life, if done for the Lord, survive and take its place in the renewed creation (perfected of course)? And second, will we work in the new heaven and new earth, or will we merely sit around playing our guitars and singing the same worship song a million times? Robert Farrar Capon sums up the usual thought about "going to heaven."

> For us, heaven is an unearthly, humanly irrelevant condition in which bed-sheeted, paper-winged spirits sit on clouds and play tinkly music until their pipe-cleaner halos drop off in boredom. As we envision it, it contains not one baby's bottom, not one woman's breast, not even one man's bare chest—much less a risen basketball game between glorified "shirts" and "skins." But in Scripture, it is a city with boys and girls playing in the streets; it is buildings put up by a Department of Public Works that uses amethysts for cinder blocks and pearls as big as the Ritz for gates; and indoors, it is a dinner party to end all dinner parties at the marriage supper of the Lamb. It is, in short, earth wedded. Not earth jilted. It is the world as the irremovable apple of God's eye.[5]

One thing is for sure. We will not be disembodied souls floating in ether, but fully resurrected persons in a beautifully renewed creation in which the invisible heaven and the visible earth have come together in a glorious union called the wedding supper of the Lamb.

---

5. Capon, *Parables of the Kingdom*, 92.

Will Our Work Last?

This is the first question we ask. We ask it in the contemporary context of the view of most Christians that only gospel work lasts. This has driven generations into full-time ministry, as though anyone could be a part-time disciple of Jesus. But, contrary to this dualistic view of work, namely that work in the church lasts and work in the world goes up in a puff of smoke, there are biblical reasons why some work in this life, done with faith, hope, and love, will last and contribute to the new heaven and new earth. So it is good to ask, is what we are doing worthy of becoming the furniture of heaven? Here are nine biblical reasons to suggest that what we do in this life, what we have made with our hands, minds, or souls, will not only survive but be glorified.

First, there is discontinuity between this life and the next, but there is also continuity. The new Jerusalem is related to this world—a city and land (Rev 21–22).

Second, the resurrected body of Jesus bore scars from this life, but they are now transfigured and become a means of faith (John 20:27). Our violent acts against nature and culture may not be erased by the final Armageddon and the final renewal but may by God's grace be transfigured. This is part of our hope. Through transcendent reasoning we can imagine that the marks we leave in this life and in this world last: open pit mines, well-manicured gardens, cedar decks, and satellite receiving stations, the good and the bad of what we are doing in this world. But there will be a transfiguration. There will be a *new* heaven and a *new* earth, really, as Jesus said, "the renewal of *all things*" (Matt 19:28, emphasis mine).[6]

Third, in the final judgment Jesus personally receives our service done in this life. "You did it to me," he will say (Matt 25:31–46).

Fourth, the apostle Paul in his Letter to the Corinthians suggests that if our work is built on Christ, the work will be saved at the end. If it is not saved the work will be burned up in the great fire at the end, though we, the worker, might be saved. "If anyone builds on this foundation [Christ] . . . their work will be shown for what it is, because the Day will bring it to light. It will be revealed with fire, and the fire will test the quality of each person's work. If what has been built survives, the builder will receive a reward. If it is burned up, the builder will suffer loss but yet will be saved—even though only as one escaping through flames" (1 Cor 3:12–15).

6. For a fuller treatment of this thought see Stevens, *Seven Days of Faith*, 43–51.

Fifth, the fire of judgment (2 Pet 3:7) does not mean annihilation but transformation (3:13). The image comprises putting raw ore into a cauldron and turning the heat up to burn out the dross. The next verse underscores that we wait for a new heaven and a new earth.

Sixth, the earth groans and waits for liberation (Rom 8:19–22). Our future is a heavenly earth or an earthly heaven.

Seventh, faith, hope, and love last, according to 1 Corinthians 13:13, though not just as isolated virtues but what is done with faith, hope, and love. A Catholic scholar, John Haughey, comments on this other occurrence of the triad of marketplace virtues.

> It seems that it is not acts of faith, hope and love in themselves that last, but rather works done in faith, hope and love: it is not the pure intention alone, nor is it faith, hope and love residing unexercised as three infused theological virtues in a person that last. What lasts is the action taken on these virtues, the praxis that flows from the intention, the works the virtues shape. These last!⁷

Eighth, the deeds of Christians follow them into the new heaven and new earth, according to Revelation 14:13.

Ninth, Paul says that our "labor in the Lord" is not in vain (1 Cor 15:58). "Always give yourself fully to the work of the Lord, because you know that your labor in the Lord is not in vain." But placed in the resurrection chapter, our labor in the Lord must be exactly what it says. N. T. Wright notes:

> In the Lord your labor is not in vain. You are following Jesus and shaping our world in the power of the Spirit; and when the final consummation comes, the work that you have done, whether in Bible study or biochemistry, whether in preaching or in pure mathematics, whether in digging ditches or in composing symphonies, will stand, will last (1 Cor 15:58).⁸

Yves Congar did much of the advance theological work in preparation for Vatican II. Congar puts the matter succinctly:

> Ontologically, this is the world that, transformed and renewed will pass into the kingdom; so . . . the dualist position is wrong; final salvation will be achieved by a wonderful refloating of our

---

7 Haughey, *Converting Nine to Five*, 106.

8. Wright, *Challenge of Jesus*, 180–81.

earthly vessel rather than the transfer of the survivors to another ship wholly built by God.[9]

But the second question is only partly answered in the last book of the Bible.

Will We Work in the New Heaven and New Earth?

There are two approaches to dealing with this question. The first is a theological. The second is textual.

First, with regard to the theological answer, we note that in the new heaven and new earth we will be fully human (including glorified bodies) rather than mere immortal souls (the Greek view of the future). In the Hebrew and biblical view of the person, the body is not an evil shell for the precious and holy soul. We do not *have* souls and bodies. We *are* bodies, *are* souls, *are* spirits. We are psychosomatic-pneumatic wholes. So, contrary to the Greek view that you get saved by getting the soul out of the body, which happens when we die, the biblical future of the human person is a glorified ensouled body or embodied soul. As fully human beings made even more into the image of God than we were in our earth-life, we will work because this is part of what it means to be made in the image of God. God is a worker, and continues to work (John 5:17). And he made us in his image as workers (Gen 1:27–28). There will be no curse to deal with, no sin, no thorns and thistles, no cantankerous customers, and no sleepless nights worrying about the bottom line. Indeed George Macdonald in his children's books envisages exchange taking place in heaven without money, and exchange is business. Each of us will be unique and have unique gifts to bring to the community of heaven. That means we are dependent on one another and must exchange what we have for what we need. And exchange is business. Two marketing professors postulate that marketers will be needed to help people make choices![10] So to be human—and we will be more human than ever—is to work.

The second answer is textual, specifically the text of Revelation. "The kings of the earth will bring their splendor into [the holy city]" (Rev 21:24). This "splendor" is the best of the culture of every nation on earth, its technology, art, literature, service, crafts, and products. Human creativity will

9. Congar, *Lay People in the Church*, 92.
10. Steen and VanderVeen, "Will There Be Marketing in Heaven?"

be expressed fully and beautifully. "The glory and honor of the nations will be brought into it" (Rev 21:26). So there will be culture creation and sharing. But more than culture, there is the activity of the people of the consummated kingdom.

These people will work. "They will reign [read: work] with him age after age after age" (Rev 22:5, *The Message*). And "the leaves of the tree [of life] are for the healing of the nations" (Rev 22:2). On each side of the river of life are not just the one tree of life, reminiscent of the garden of Eden, but the *trees* of life. And the leaves of the tree are for the healing of the nations. Sometimes doctors say to me there will be no work for them in heaven. Here is what I answer. Whatever gifts, talents, and personality you have now will be present and exalted in the new heaven and new earth. Indeed, your calling, which I assume is to help people, does not end with death, or worse still with formal retirement. It continues into eternity. And what if all heaven is healing and renewal? And what if your gifts and talents find new expression in the context of the presence of God and the love community of the Lamb?

And who would not want to be there? Speaking many years ago at a course at Regent College, Clark Pinnock read from 1 Corinthians: "What no eye has seen, what no ear has heard, and what no human mind has conceived—the things God has prepared for those who love him—these are the things God has revealed to us by the Spirit" (1 Cor 2:9–10). Then, Pinnock, through his tears, said: "It like this. A little girl wants a baby doll for her Christmas present. But what she is given is a living baby sister."

W. H. Auden, while introducing Charles Williams's novel *The Descent of the Dove*, put it starkly:

> Charles Williams succeeds, where even Dante, I think, fails, in showing us that nobody is ever *sent* to Hell; he, or she, insists on going there. If, as Christians believe, God is love, then, in one sense, he is not omnipotent, for He cannot compel His creatures to accept His Love without ceasing to be Himself. The wrath of God is not *His* wrath but the way in which those feel His Love who refuse it, and the right of refusal is a privilege which not even their Creator can take from them.[11]

No one is ever sent to hell. I take this to be a fairly good translation of the statement of Jesus in the Gospel of John: "This is the verdict [judgment]: Light has come into the world, but people loved darkness instead of light

11. Williams, *Descent of the Dove*, viii.

because their deeds were evil" (John 3:19). In other words, people judge themselves in the presence of the light of the kingdom and the King. Some insist on going to hell. Why? Because heaven is permeated with the presence of God whom we will see face to face and to know as we are known.

Yes, creativity will be there. Yes, humanity will be there. Yes, work will be there. But best of all, God and the people of God from every race, culture, and background will be there. And I use the term "there" because it will be a place. And also some of the things we have done—relational, instrumental, medical, domestic, service, and construction work—will have eternity kneaded into it. We will continue to work—with joy. Rudyard Kipling, the British poet, envisioned it this way:

> WHEN Earth's last picture is painted and the tubes are twisted and dried,
> When the oldest colours have faded, and the youngest critic has died,
> We shall rest, and, faith, we shall need it—lie down for an æon or two,
> Till the Master of All Good Workmen shall put us to work anew.
> And those that were good shall be happy: they shall sit in a golden chair;
> They shall splash at a ten-league canvas with brushes of comets' hair.
> They shall find real saints to draw from—Magdalene, Peter, and Paul;
> They shall work for an age at a sitting and never be tired at all!
> And only the Master shall praise us, and only the Master shall blame;
> And no one shall work for money, and no one shall work for fame,
> But each for the joy of the working, and each, in his separate star,
> Shall draw the Thing as he sees It for the God of Things as They are![12]

I add in conclusion: Our working clothes in the consummated kingdom will be white, or at least that is what is suggested by the last vision of the Bible—the grand rendezvous: "Fine linen, bright and clean, were given her to wear" (Rev 19:8).

12. Kipling, "When Earth's Last Picture Was Painted."

Bibliography

Allen, Roland. *Missionary Methods: St Paul's or Ours?* Grand Rapids: Eerdmans, 1961.

Anderson, Ray. *Minding God's Business.* Grand Rapids: Eerdmans, 1986.

Alexander, Irene, and Christopher Brown, eds. *To Whom Shall We Go? Faith Responses in a Time of Crisis.* Eugene, OR: Wipf and Stock, 2021.

Alter, K. S. *Managing the Double Bottom Line.* Washington, DC: Pact, 2000.

Arias, Mortimer. *Announcing the Reign of God: Evangelization and the Subversive Memory of Jesus.* Eugene, OR: Wipf and Stock, 2001.

Arnold, Clinton E. *Powers of Darkness: Principalities and Powers in Paul's Letters.* Downers Grove, IL: InterVarsity, 1992.

Baker, Dwight. "Missional Geometry: Plotting the Coordinates of Business as Mission." In *Business as Mission: From Impoverished to Empowered*, edited by Tom Steffan and Mike Barnett, 42–54. Evangelical Missiological Society Series 14. Pasadena, CA: William Carey Library, 2006.

Bakke, Dennis W. *Joy at Work: A Revolutionary Approach to Fun on the Job.* Seattle: PVG, 2005.

Banks, Robert. "Blessing." In *The Complete Book of Everyday Christianity*, edited by Robert Banks and R. Paul Stevens, 72–74. Downers Grove, IL: InterVarsity, 1997.

———. *God the Worker: Journeys into the Mind, Heart, and Imagination of God.* Claremont, CA: Albatross, 1992.

———. *Faith Goes to Work: Reflections from the Marketplace.* Eugene, OR: Wipf and Stock, 1999.

Barclay, William. *Flesh and Spirit: An Examination of Galatians 5:19–23.* London: SCM, 1962.

Behr, John. *Becoming Human: Meditations on Christian Anthropology in Word and Image.* Crestwood, NY: St. Vladimir's Seminary Press, 2013.

Benedict XVI. *What It Means to Be a Christian.* https://books.google.com/books/about/What_it_Means_to_be_a_Christian.html?id=L41HDwAAQBAJ.

Benson, Iain. "Values." In *The Complete Book of Everyday Christianity*, edited by Robert Banks and R. Paul Stevens, 1064–66. Downers Grove, IL: InterVarsity, 1997.

———. "Virtues." In *The Complete Book of Everyday Christianity*, edited by Robert Banks and R. Paul Stevens, 1069–72. Downers Grove, IL: InterVarsity, 1997.

Berger, Peter L. *The Sacred Canopy: Elements of a Sociological Theory of Religion.* Garden City, NY: Doubleday and Co., 1967.

Blake, William. "A Vision of the Last Judgment." In *William Blake's Writings*, Vol. II, edited by G. E. Bentley Jr., 1007–28. Oxford: Clarendon, 1978.

Block, Peter. *Stewardship: Choosing Service Over Self-Interest.* San Francisco: Berrett & Koehler, 2013.

Boersma, Hans. *Heavenly Participation: The Weaving of a Sacramental Tapestry.* 1st ed. Grand Rapids: Eerdmans, 2011.

Bonhoeffer, Dietrich. *No Rusty Swords: Letters Lectures and Notes 1928–1936.* The Collected Works of Dietrich Bonhoeffer, vol. 1. New York: Harper & Row, 1965.

Bonino, J. M. *Doing Theology in a Revolutionary Situation.* Philadelphia: Fortress, 1975.

Bosch, David J. *Transforming Mission: Paradigm Shifts in the Theology of Mission.* Maryknoll, NY: Orbis, 1991.

Bright, John. *The Kingdom of God.* Nashville: Abingdon, 1953.

Buchanan, C. O. "Sacrament." In *New Dictionary of Theology,* edited by Sinclair B. Ferguson and David F. Wright, 606–8. Downers Grove, IL: InterVarsity, 1988.

Capon, Robert Farrar. *An Offering of Uncles.* New York: Harper & Row, 1969.

———. *The Parables of the Kingdom.* Grand Rapids: Eerdmans, 1985.

Caragounis, Chrys C. D. "Kingdom of God/Heaven." In Joel Green, Scot McKnight, and I. Howard Marshall, eds., *Dictionary of Jesus and the Gospels,* 417–30. Downers Grove, IL: InterVarsity, 1992.

Carey, William. *An Enquiry into the Obligations of Christians to Use Means for the Conversion of the Heathens.* London: Carey Kingsgate, 1792.

Charles, J. Daryl. *Wisdom and Work: Theological Reflections on Human Labor from Ecclesiastes.* Eugene, OR: Cascade, 2021.

Collins, Phil, and Stevens, R. Paul. *The Equipping Pastor: A Systems Approach to Congregational Leadership.* Washington, DC: Alban Institute, 1993.

Congar, Yves. *Lay People in the Church: A Study for a Theology of the Laity.* Translated by D. Attwater. Westminster, MD: Newman, 1957.

Cosden, Darrell. *The Heavenly Good of Earthly Work.* Peabody, MA: Hendrickson, 2006.

Costa, John Dalla. *Magnificence at Work: Living Faith in Business.* Ottawa: Novalis, 2005.

Crawford, Matthew B. *Shop Class As Soulcraft: An Inquiry into the Value of Work.* New York: Penguin, 2009.

———. *The World Beyond Your Head: On Becoming an Individual in an Age of Distraction.* New York: Farrar, Straus, and Giroux, 2015.

Dale, Eric Steven. *Bringing Heaven Down to Earth: A Practical Spirituality of Work.* New York: Peter Lang, 1991.

Daniels, Denise, and Shannon Vandewarker. *Working in the Presence of God: Spiritual Practices for Everyday Work.* Peabody, MA: Hendrickson, 2019.

Davis, John Jefferson. "'Teaching Them to Observe All that I Have Commanded You': The History of the Interpretation of the 'Great Commission' and Implications for Marketplace Ministries." South Hamilton, MA: Gordon-Conwell Theological Seminary, unpublished, 1998.

De Pree, Max. *Leadership Is an Art.* New York: Doubleday, 1989.

Deissmann, Adolf. *Paul: A Study in Social and Religious History.* Translated by W. E. Wilson. New York: George H. Duran, 1926.

Dickson, John. *Humilitas: A Lost Key to Life, Love, and Leadership.* Grand Rapids: Zondervan, 2011.

Diehl, William E., and Judith Ruhe Diehl. *It Ain't Over Till It's Over.* Minneapolis: Augsburg, 2003.

Dumbrell, William. *Covenant and Creation.* Nashville: Thomas Nelson, 1984.

———. "Creation, Covenant and Work." *Crux* vol. XXIV, no. 3 (September 1988) 14–24.

———. *End of the Beginning: Revelation 21–22 and the Old Testament.* Homebush West, NSW: Lancer, 1985.

———. "The End of the Beginning: Revelation 21–22 and the Old Testament." The Moore College Lectures 1984. *Themelios* 15:2. https://www.thegospelcoalition. org/themelios/review/the-end-of-the-beginning-revelation-21-22-and-the-old-testament/.

Eldred, Ken. *God Is at Work: Transforming People and Nations Through Business.* Ventura, CA: Regal, 2005.

Ellul, Jacques. *The Presence of the Kingdom.* New York: Seabury, 1967.

Erisman, Albert M. *The Accidental Executive: Lessons on Business, Faith, and Calling from the Life of Joseph.* Peabody, MA: Hendrickson, 2015.

Fischer, R. H. "Luther on the Priesthood of All Believers." *The Baptist Quarterly* 17 (July 1958) 293–311.

Forsyth, P. T. *Positive Preaching and the Modern Mind.* Grand Rapids: Eerdmans, 1964.

France, R. T. *Divine Government: God's Kingship in the Gospel of Mark.* London: SPCK, 1990.

———. *Matthew.* Tyndale New Testament Commentaries. Grand Rapids: Eerdmans, 1985.

Galilea, Segundo. *The Way of Living Faith: A Spirituality of Liberation.* Quezon City, Philippines: Claretion, 1982.

Garber, Steven. *The Seamless Life: A Tapestry of Love and Learning, Worship and Work.* Downers Grove, IL: InterVarsity, 2020.

Gillespie, Thomas W. "The Laity in Biblical Perspective." *Theology Today* 36:3 (October 1979) 315–27.

Goossen, Richard J., and R. Paul Stevens. *Entrepreneurial Leadership: Finding Your Calling, Making a Difference.* Downers Grove, IL: InterVarsity, 2013.

Goslinga, C. J. *Joshua, Judges, Ruth.* Grand Rapids: Zondervan, 1986.

Grayson, Rob. "Faith Meets World: Reflections on faith in a messed-up but beautiful world." Blog. https://www.faithmeetsworld.com/review-kingdom-conspiracy-by-scot-mcknight/.

Green, Michael. *Evangelism in the Early Church.* Grand Rapids: Eerdmans, 2000.

Greenleaf, Robert. *Servant Leadership: A Journey into the Nature of Legitimate Power and Greatness.* Mahwah, NJ: Paulist, 1977.

Gunton, Colin. *The One, the Three and the Many: God, Creation and the Culture of Modernity.* Cambridge: Cambridge University Press, 1993.

Hamilton, James M. *Work: And Our Labor in the Lord.* Wheaton, IL: Crossway, 2017.

Hardy, Lee. *The Fabric of This World: Inquiries into Calling, Career Choice, and the Design of Human Work.* Grand Rapids: Eerdmans, 1990.

Harkness, Georgia. *The Church and Its Laity.* New York: Abingdon, 1962.

Haughey, John. *Converting Nine to Five: A Spirituality of Daily Work.* New York: Crossroads, 1989.

Holland, Joe. *Creative Communion: Toward a Spirituality of Work.* Mahwah, NJ: Paulist, 1989.

Jensen, David H. *Responsive Labor: A Theology of Work.* Louisville: Westminster John Knox, 2006.

Jeremias, Joachim. *The Parables of Jesus.* Rev. ed. London: SCM, 1972.

John Paul II. *On Human Work.* Boston: St. Paul Editions, 1981.

Johnson, Darrell W. *The Beatitudes: Living in Sync with the Reign of God.* Vancouver, BC: Regent College Publishing, 2015.

Johnson, C. Neal. *Business as Mission: A Comprehensive Guide to Theory and Practice.* Downers Grove: IVP Academic, 2009.

———. "Toward a Marketplace Missiology." *Missiology* 31:1 (January 2003) 87–95.

Johnson, C. Neal, and Steve Rundle. "Distinctives and Challenges of Business as Mission." In *Business as Missio: From Impoverished to Empowered,* edited by Tom Steffan and Mike Barnett, 19–36. Evangelical Missiological Society Series 14, 2006.

Jordan-Smith, Paul. "Seven (and more) Deadly Sins." *Parabola* 10 (Winter 1985) 34–45.

Kaemingk, Matthew. "Lesslie Newbigin's Missional Approach to the Marketplace," *Missiology: An International Review* vol. XXXIX, no. 3 (July 2011) 323–33.

Kaemingk, Matthew, and Cory B. Willson. *Work and Worship: Connecting Our Labor and Liturgy.* Grand Rapids: Baker, 2020.

Keller, Timothy, and Katherine Leary Alsdorf. *Every Good Endeavor: Connecting Your Work to God's Work.* New York: Dutton/Penguin Group, 2012.

Kidner, Derek. *Psalms 1–72: An Introduction and Commentary.* Downers Grove, IL: InterVarsity, 1973.

Kipling, Rudyard. "When Earth's Last Picture Was Painted." Bartleby.com/364/124.html.

Klappert, Berthold. "King, Kingdom." In *The New International Dictionary of New Testament Theology, vol. 2,* edited by Lothar Coenen, Erich Beyreuther, and Hans Bietenhard, 372–90. Grand Rapids: Zondervan, 1969.

Kraybill, Donald B. *The Upside-Down Kingdom.* Scottsdale, PA: Herald, 2003.

Kroeker, Wally. "Dangerous to the Status Quo." *The Marketplace: MEDA's Magazine for Christians in Business* (January–February 2001) 2.

Ladd, George Eldon. *The Gospel of the Kingdom: Popular Expositions on the Kingdom of God.* Grand Rapids: Eerdmans, 1959.

Laing, R. D. *The Politics of Experience and the Bird of Paradise.* Harmondsworth, UK: Penguin, 1970.

Leech, Kenneth. *Experiencing God: Theology as Spirituality.* San Francisco: Harper & Row, 1985.

———. *True Prayer: An Invitation to Christian Spirituality.* San Francisco: Harper & Row, 1980.

Leith, John H., ed. *Creeds of the Churches.* New York: Anchor, 1963.

MacLeod, George. *Only One Way Left.* Glasgow: The Iona Community, 1956.

Marshall, I. Howard. "Son of Man." In *Dictionary of Jesus and the Gospels,* edited by Joel Green, Scot McKnight, and I. Howard Marshall, 775–81. Downers Grove, IL: InterVarsity, 1992.

McKnight, Scot. "Church and Kingdom: Let's Get Our Analogies Straight." *Regent World* 27:1 (January 21, 2015) 1.

Meilander, Gilbert C., ed. *Working: Its Meaning and Its Limits.* Notre Dame, IN: University of Notre Dame: 2000.

Miller, Hal. "Success." In *The Complete Book of Everyday Christianity,* edited by Robert Banks and R. Paul Stevens, 988–91. Downers Grove, IL: InterVarsity, 1997.

Moltmann, Jürgen. *The Trinity and the Kingdom.* Translated by Margaret Kohl. San Francisco: Harper & Row, 1991.

Motyer, J. Alec. *The Prophecy of Isaiah: An Introduction & Commentary.* Downers Grove, IL: InterVarsity, 1993.

Muggeridge, Malcolm. *Jesus Rediscovered.* London: Collins, 1969.

Murray, Andrew. *Like Christ*. New York: Hurst and Co., n.d.

Newbigin, Lesslie. *Honest Religion for Secular Man*. Philadelphia: Westminster, 1966.

———. *Signs Amid the Rubble: The Purpose of God in Human History*. Grand Rapids: Eerdmans, 2003.

Novak, Michael. *Business as a Calling: Work and the Examined Life*. New York: Free Press, 1996.

Nygren, Anders. "Luther's Doctrine of the Two Kingdoms." *Ecumenical Review* 1:3 (April 1949) 301–10.

Oliver, Edmund H. *The Social Achievements of the Christian Church*. Vancouver, BC: Regent College Publishing, 2004.

Pennington, Jonathan T. *The Sermon on the Mount and Human Flourishing: A Theological Commentary*. Grand Rapids: Baker Academic, 2017.

———. "Human Flourishing and the Bible." In *Counting the Cost: Christian Perspectives on Capitalism*, edited by Art Lindsley and Anne R. Bradley, 44–46. Abilene, TX: Abilene Christian University Press, 2017.

Perkins, William. *A Golden Chain* (1592). In *The Courtenay Library of Reformation Classics*, III, *The Work of William Perkins*, edited by I. Breward. Appleford, UK: Sutton Courtenay, 1970.

———. "Treatise on Vocations." In *The Works of William Perkins*, Vol. 10, edited by Joseph A. Piper and J. Yuille, 31–107. Grand Rapids: Reformational Heritage, 2020.

———. *The Works of That Famous Minister of Christ in the University of Cambridge*. London: John Legatt, 1626.

Pierce, Gregory F. A. *Spirituality at Work: 10 Ways to Balance Your Life on the Job*. Chicago: Loyola, 2001.

Pink, Daniel H. *A Whole New Mind: Why Right-Brainers Will Rule the Future*. New York: Riverhead, 2006.

Plantinga, Cornelius, Jr. *Not the Way It's Supposed to Be: A Breviary of Sin*. Grand Rapids, Eerdmans, 1996.

Pollay, Richard, and R. Paul Stevens. "Advertising." In *The Complete Book of Everyday Christianity*, edited by Robert Banks and R. Paul Stevens, 23–27. Downers Grove, IL: InterVarsity, 1997.

Preece, Gordon. *Changing Work Values: A Christian Response*. Melbourne: Acorn, 1995.

Richardson, Alan. *The Biblical Doctrine of Work*. London: SCM, 1954.

Riefenstahl, Leni, dir. *The Triumph of the Will*. 1935. www.synapse-films.com.

Ryken, Leland. *Work and Leisure in Christian Perspective*. Eugene, OR: Wipf and Stock, 2002.

Sayson, David. "The Church Fathers and IMT." Presentation to IMT Fellows Plus, Vancouver, BC, November 6, 2020.

Schleir, Heinrich. *Principalities and Powers in the New Testament*. New York: Herder and Herder, 1964.

Schmemann, Alexander. *For the Life of the World: Sacraments and Orthodoxy*. Crestwood, NY: St Vladimir's Seminary Press, 1988.

Schumacher, Christian. *God in Work: Discovering the Divine Pattern for Work in the New Millennium*. Oxford: Lion, 1998.

Sempangi, Kefa. "Walking in the Light." *Sojourners*, July 1981.

Sherman, Amy L. *Kingdom Calling: Vocational Stewardship for the Common Good*. Downers Grove, IL: InterVarsity, 2011.

Sherman, Doug, and William Hendricks. *Your Work Matters to God*. Colorado Springs, CO: NavPress, 1987.

Silvoso, Ed. *Anointed for Business: How Christians Can Use Their Influence in the Marketplace to Change the World*. Ventura, CA: Regal, 2002.

Smith, James Byran. *The Magnificent Story*. Downers Grove, IL: InterVarsity, 2017.

Snyder, Howard. *The Community of the King*. Downers Grove, IL: InterVarsity, 2004.

Stackhouse, Max L., Dennis P. McCann, Shirley J. Roles, and Preston N. Williams, eds. *On Moral Business: Classical and Contemporary Resources for Ethics in Economic Life*. Grand Rapids: Eerdmans. 1995.

Steen, Todd, and Steve VanderVeen. "Will There Be Marketing in Heaven?" *Perspectives* (November 2003) 6–11.

Steffen, Tom, and Mike Barnett, eds. *Business as Mission: From Impoverished to Empowered*. Evangelical Missiological Society Series. Pasadena, CA: William Carey Library, 2006.

Stevens, Mark A., ed. *Webster's New Explorer Desk Encyclopedia*. Springfield, MA: Merriam-Webster, 2003.

Stevens, R. Paul. *The Abolition of the Laity: Vocation, Work and Ministry in Biblical Perspective*. Carlisle, UK: Paternoster, 1999.

———. "The Covenant Mandate—An Approach to the Theology of the Laity." Unpublished, Regent College, 1989.

———. *Doing God's Business: Meaning and Motivation for the Marketplace*. Grand Rapids: Eerdmans, 2006.

———. *The Equipper's Guide to Every-Member Ministry*. Downers Grove, IL: InterVarsity, 1993.

———. *The Other Six Days: Vocation, Work, and Ministry in Biblical Perspective*. Grand Rapids: Eerdmans, 1999.

———. "Poems for People in Distress: The Apocalypse of John and the Contemplative Life," *Themelios* 18 (January 1993) 11–14.

———. *Seven Days of Faith*. 2nd ed. Eugene, OR: Cascade, 2021.

———. "Soul." In *The Complete Book of Everyday Christianity*, edited by Robert Banks and R. Paul Stevens, 922–26. Downers Grove, IL: InterVarsity, 1997.

———. *Work Matters: Lessons from Scripture*. Grand Rapids: Eerdmans, 2012.

Stevens, R. Paul, and Clive Lim. *Money Matters: Faith, Life and Wealth*. Grand Rapids: Eerdmans, 2021.

Stevens, R. Paul, and Alvin Ung. *Taking Your Soul to Work: Overcoming the Nine Deadly Sins of the Workplace*. Grand Rapids: Eerdmans, 2010.

Stewart, James. *A Faith to Proclaim*. London: Hodder and Stoughton, 1953.

Sweeden, Joshua R. *The Church and Work: The Ecclesiastical Grounding of Good Work*. Eugene, OR: Pickwick, 2014.

Tan, Kim. *The Jubilee Gospel: The Jubilee, Spirit and the Church*. Colorado Springs, CO: Authentic, 2008.

Thompson, Marianne Meye. *Colossians and Philemon*. The Two Horizons New Testament Commentary. Grand Rapids: Eerdmans, 2005.

Torrance, Thomas F. *Trinitarian Perspectives: Toward Doctrinal Agreement*. Edinburgh: T. & T. Clark, 1994.

Trueblood, Elton. *The Common Ventures of Life*. New York: Harper and Bros., 1949.

Van Duzer, Jeff. *Why Business Matters to God: And What Still Needs to Be Fixed*. Downers Grove, IL: InterVarsity Academic, 2010.

Van Sloten, John. *Every Job a Parable: What Walmart Greeters, Nurses & Astronauts Tell Us about God.* Colorado Springs, CO: NavPress, 2017.

Vest, Norlene. *Friend of the Soul: A Benedictine Spirituality of Work.* Cambridge, MA: Cowley, 1997.

Volf, Miroslav. "Human Work, Divine Spirit, and the New Creation: Toward a Pneumatological Understanding of Work." *Pneuma: The Journal of the Society for Pentecostal Studies* (Fall 1987) 173–93.

———. *Work in the Spirit: Toward a Theology of Work.* Oxford: Oxford University Press, 1991.

Waltke, Bruce K. *Genesis: A Commentary.* Grand Rapids: Zondervan, 2001.

———. *Old Testament Theology.* Grand Rapids: Zondervan, 2007.

Weil, Simone. *Waiting on God: The Essence of Her Thought.* Translated by Emma Craufurd. London: Fontana, 1959.

Whelchel, Hugh. *How Then Should We Work? Rediscovering the Biblical Doctrine of Work.* Bloomington, IN: West Bow, 2012.

Williams, Charles. *The Descent of the Dove: A History of the Holy Spirit in the Church.* New York: Meridian, 1956.

Wink, Walter. *Naming the Powers: The Language of Power in the New Testament.* Philadelphia: Fortress, 1984.

Witherington, Ben, III. *Work: A Kingdom Perspective on Labor.* Grand Rapids: Eerdmans, 2011.

Wolff, H. W. *Anthropology of the Old Testament.* Translated by M. Kohl. Philadelphia: Fortress, 1981.

Wright, Christopher. "Integral Mission and the Great Commission: 'The Five Marks of Mission.'" 2014. https://www.loimission.net/wp-content/uploads/2014/03/Chris-Wright-IntegralMissionandtheGreatCommission.pdf.

Wright, N. T. *After You Believe: Why Christian Character Matters.* San Francisco: HarperOne, 2012.

———. *The Challenge of Jesus: Rediscovering Who Jesus Was and Is.* Downers Grove, IL: InterVarsity, 1999.

———. "Jesus." In *The New Testament Dictionary of Theology,* edited by Sinclair B. Ferguson, David F. Wright, and J. I. Packer, 348–51. Downers Grove, IL: InterVarsity, 1988.

———. *Surprised by Hope: Rethinking Heaven, the Resurrection, and the Mission of the Church.* New York: HarperOne, 2008.

Wyszynski, Stefan Cardinal. *All You Who Labor: Work and the Sanctification of Daily Life.* Manchester, NH: Sophia Institute, 1995.

Yamamori, Tetsunao, and Kenneth A. Eldred, eds. *On Kingdom Business: Transforming Missions Through Entrepreneurial Strategies.* Wheaton, IL: Crossway, 2003.

Index of Ancient Documents

Index of Subjects

Made in the USA
Coppell, TX
19 January 2023

11405250R00132